Discovering The Cotswolds

Other titles in this series

Discovering
The Cotswolds

CHARLES W. J. WITHERS

JOHN DONALD PUBLISHERS LTD
EDINBURGH

To my children
James, Claire, Christopher

© Charles W. J. Withers 1990

ISBN 0 85976 268 8

Phototypesetting by Newtext Composition Ltd, Glasgow
Printed and bound in Great Britain by Martins of Berwick

Acknowledgements

A number of friends and colleagues have given freely of their advice and constructive criticism in the writing of this book, and I am grateful to them. I am particularly grateful to Nick Chidlaw and Mike Field in this respect, to Penguin Books for allowing me to use Verey's volume to check facts regarding Cotswold architecture, and to the staff of the libraries at the College of St Paul and St Mary, Cheltenham Public Library, and Gloucestershire County Record Office.

For the illustrations which appear on pages 61, 69, 91, 101, 107, 109, 113, 127, 137, 149, 159, 163, 167, 169, and 187, I am grateful to the Gloucestershire County Record Office for their help in research and permission to reproduce them here. For permission to reproduce the illustration on page 179, I acknowledge Mr Humphrey Household; and for permission to reproduce that on page 127, I am grateful to Mr P. Griffiths and the Cotswolds Postcard Collectors' Club. The plates on pages 25, 27, 49, and 55 are reproduced with the kind permission of the University of Cambridge Committee for Aerial Photography. I acknowledge with thanks Mr P. D. Turner for the illustrations which appear on pages 17, 57, 87, and 161; Mrs Wynne-Jones of Barnsley for permission to use the photograph on page 155; the family of the late Mr R. W. Paterson and the County Record Office for the picture on page 181. The illustrations which appear on pages 26, 73, 77, and 151 do so through the courtesy of the Gloucestershire Echo. The maps and tables on pages viii, 6, 7, 21, 31, 66, and 67 were drawn by Sheila Taylor; the map on page 51 includes material from maps compiled by R. E. Glasscock from records of the Medieval Village Research Group and drawn by M. Young, Department of Geography, Cambridge University. Steve Randall helped with the reproduction of other illustrations. I acknowledge the help of Steven Blake and Cheltenham Art Gallery and Museums in including the cartoon on page 85. For the colour illustrations, I am grateful to the Rev. Bell of

Fairford, Cheltenham Tourist Information Centre, the University of Cambridge Committee for Aerial Photography, and especially to Paul Felix.

Debts are due also to all those Cotswold folk who have helped in any way; not least to Anne, my wife, for reading drafts; and to John Tuckwell for his encouragement and friendship.

C.W.J.W.

Contents

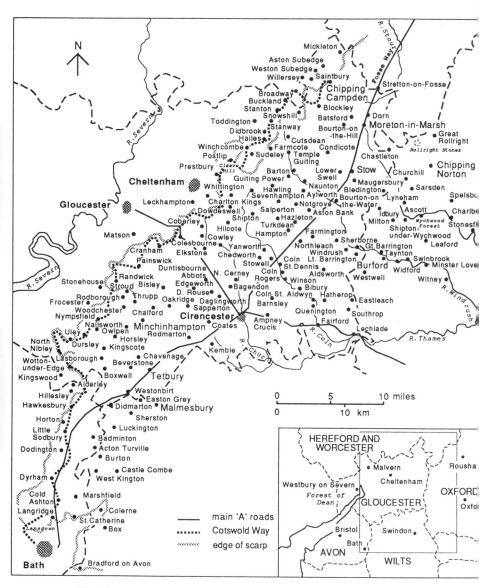

The Cotswolds, showing places mentioned in the text.

Introduction

The Cotswolds are that sweep of rounded hills and valleys lying between the Midland vales and the south-west of England. No precise administrative definition exists for this upland area of limestone and the characteristic countryside and architecture it has produced. The Cotswolds lie chiefly in Gloucestershire, but south-western margins embrace parts of Wiltshire and Avon and to the north and east extend into Worcestershire and Oxfordshire respectively. In what follows, the Cotswolds have been defined as all that lies within the roughly kite-shaped area bounded by Chipping Campden to the north, Burford to the east, Stroud to the west, and Bradford-on-Avon to the south. Where the book ranges beyond these limits, it is partly to incorporate particular places of interest and partly because the Cotswolds will never permit of formal definition anyway.

The Cotswolds lie toward the south-western end of that broad band of gently eastward-dipping Jurassic limestone that runs across England from near Lyme Regis in Dorset to the Humber estuary. The general form of this limestone ridge helps explain the two principal types of scenery found in the Cotswolds. The eastward-sloping hills and valleys are the 'wolds' proper, a 'fat' landscape of farms, villages, and gentle hills. In contrast the more steeply-inclined western edge reaches 900 feet above sea level in places, and, although eaten into by wooded river valleys, runs almost unbroken for over fifty miles. At the foot of the western scarp and along the valleys lie towns and villages whose past has been more industrial than the principally agricultural eastern wolds.

Yet, however different the historical experience of given places, the Cotswolds as a region has a unity of character and style. This unity is based upon the widespread use in building of Cotswold stone. Cotswold limestone, although it has localised tones and variations in texture, is predominantly honey-yellow in colour when freshly exposed. It weathers to a creamy grey-yellow. Local stone has been used throughout the Cotswolds for a variety of purposes – long barrows, barns, mills, eighteenth-century field boundaries as well as houses and

1

churches – and it is this continuing tradition in stone and style that gives the region its identity.

The name 'Cotswolds' was originally applied to a much smaller area. The name is derived from the Saxon personal name 'Cod' (pronounced 'Code'). Cod established a small settlement in a clearing on what was then heavily wooded country north of Winchcombe. 'Cot's dene', his house in a clearing, is now the village of Cutsdean, and the term 'Cot's wolds', used of the hills in the immediate locality, is now used of a much wider area. The inhabitants are generally known as 'Cotsallers' although local identities in given valleys and villages are also strongly maintained.

In large part, this book is an attempt to discover – by being in and looking at them – the Cotswolds of today: particular places, interesting and important buildings to visit, walks to take and things to do and see. In part also, it tries to go beyond or perhaps 'beneath' the landscape as it is now to understand the processes by which the Cotswolds have come to wear their present face. The present is a necessary beginning for all discoverers, of course, but the Cotswolds is a region of considerable historical continuity within contemporary change. What we can now see – Iron Age hillforts, for example, prehistoric trackways, Anglo-Saxon churches, the sites of deserted medieval villages, old railway cuttings, disused mills – are remnants of past Cotswolds landscapes. Discovering these former Cotswolds means knowing quite what it is of the past we're looking at in the present, and this book is intended to help the discoverer to both look and know.

In balancing description and explanation, decisions have been taken which affect the structure and organisation of the material. Given the book's modest proportions, no attempt has been made to be all-embracing. Not all villages and places are mentioned, not all themes receive equal coverage. The towns and larger villages have been covered by a short urban trail: extended town trails and guides are available from most relevant Tourist Information Offices.

Chapters 1 to 8 are largely chronological in intent, and move from geology, through the archaeology and peopling of the Cotswolds, to the more recent past and the modern landscape. Within these chapters, attention is paid to particular themes

Not all Cotswold signs are as confusing as this way marker to the Oxfordshire Way in Ascott-under-Wychwood (301189) in the eastern wolds!

which, at given moments and in certain places, have been important in shaping the character of the region. Chapters 9 to 22 are principally topographical. Questions of ease of access and distance between places have partly influenced the order of these chapters (although it is true that nowhere is very far from anywhere else in the Cotswolds, either in time or distance). Each of these chapters and the places listed and discussed might form the basis to a day's touring and sightseeing. Some parts of the Cotswolds and some places will need more than one day to be fully explored, of course, and neither chapter order nor contents is intended to prescribe or proscribe how you should discover the region. The balance of chronological, thematic, and topographical approaches should allow some planning ahead by the more organised tourist, however, as well as explain the principal features of any place or period for those with less time to spend. Ordinary road or touring maps will be of limited value here. The best maps to use are the Ordnance Survey 1:50,000 sheets (the Landranger Series), although the more detailed but less commonly-available maps at 1:25,000 scale have a wealth of topographical detail not shown on maps of larger scale. Sheets 151 and 163 in the Landranger 1:50,000 series cover most of the Cotswolds and together should be sufficient for most purposes. A number of places on the fringes of the region are covered by adjacent map sheets: 150, 162, 164, 172, and 173. All these maps are easily obtainable at bookshops and some newsagents. Places of interest are given a grid reference, to six figures, to aid discovery. For those unfamiliar with grid references, each map is divided into a grid with vertical lines, 'eastings' as they are known, and horizontal lines or 'northings'. Each place both falls within a square within this grid and has a unique location found by estimating, in tenths, its position. Thus, Winchcombe on map sheet 163 lies in grid square 02 (easting) and 28 (northing). Its actual position to six figures is (025285).

What follows is neither a practical guide to times and days of opening of general tourist facilities nor a specialised handbook for walkers, archaeologists, or architectural historians. Particular guides and maps exist for the latter groups, Tourist Information Offices for the former. No recommendations (or instructions to avoid) are given for hotels, inns, or pubs unless for their architectural or historical interest. After all, tracing culinary contours should be part of discovering and finding delight in any region.

CHAPTER 1

'The Rocks Beneath': the Geology of the Cotswolds

The rocks that make up the Cotswolds are Jurassic in age, deposited between 190 and 140 million years ago as sediments in warm shallow seas. The Jurassic succession in the Cotswolds is dominated by limestones, marls and mudrocks with subordinate sandstones. Human occupancy of the Cotswolds has been greatly influenced by this underlying geology and the topography resulting from its varied erosion. The geological structure of the Cotswolds is reasonably straightforward. The inter-layered series of limestones, marls, and mudrocks have been tilted towards the south-east. The sequence of Upper, Middle, and Lower Jurassic rocks represented but not always visible in the Cotswolds is shown in the accompanying table and their geographical distribution may be seen from the map. Lower Lias clays form cold and heavy vale soils to the foot of the western scarp. Thin limestones occur in layers particularly towards the base of the clays. It is said that the term 'Lias' was adopted by William Smith, the eighteenth-century geologist born in Churchill (283243) in the Oxfordshire wolds, who borrowed it from Cotswold quarriers for whom these stone 'liers' (layers) were used in flooring.

Moving upwards in the geological column and into younger rocks as we do so, the Lower Lias is succeeded by the Middle Lias. This is principally characterised by the Dyrham Silts and the harder Marlstone Rock Bed. The Marlstone Rock Bed, which rarely exceeds fifteen feet in thickness along its length, is relatively resistant to erosion in comparison with rocks above and below. The result of this differential erosion is that the Marlstone Rock Bed stands out as a platform, the Cotswold sub-edge. This platform in places gives rich soils used as meadow but the sub-edge has also been heavily wooded in the past. Where iron hydroxides in the Marlstone outweigh carbonates, iron ores have been worked as at Iron Acton (677837), near Chipping Sodbury. The iron-rich character of

5

Series	Group		Formation
Upper Jurassic			Oxford Clay Kellaways Clay and Sand
Middle Jurassic	Great Oolite		Cornbrash Limestone Forest Marble Complex of Limestone and Clay (including Fullers' Earth) formations
	Inferior Oolite		Upper Inferior Oolite Middle Inferior Oolite Lower Inferior Oolite
Lower Jurassic	Lias	Upper	Cephalopod Bed (S.Cotswolds) Upper Lias Clay/Cotteswold Sands
		Middle	Marlstone Rock Bed Dyrham Silt
		Lower	Lower Lias Clay White and Blue Lias Limestone

The geological succession in the Cotswolds.

the Middle Lias Marlstone in the north-east Cotswolds gives rock there the name 'ironstone', and the district around Wychwood Forest (335173) is known as 'Ironstone Country'.

The Upper Lias occurs as a fairly narrow outcrop in the steeper parts of the north-east to south-west trending Jurassic scarp. Much of the Upper Lias is silts and fine sands known collectively as the Cotswold (or Cotteswold) Sands. Near Stinchcombe (734987), these sands have a thickness of 230 feet. To the south they are overlain by fossil-rich sediments known as the Cephalopod Beds because of the wealth of ammonites and belemnites they contain. To the north, the Cotswold Sands thin out and give way to Upper Lias clays. This varying conjunction of clays and sands is an important influence upon sites of settlement since groundwater is forced out as springs where the rock types meet.

On top of the Lias lies the Middle Jurassic oolitic limestone, the stone whose colour is most associated with the Cotswolds scene. The word 'oolite' derives from the Greek *oön* and *lithos,* literally 'egg-stone'. Oolitic limestone consists chiefly of small

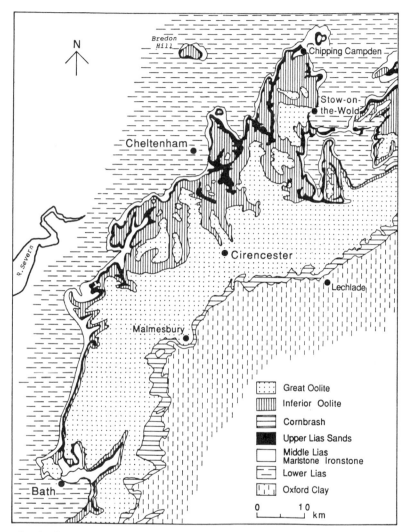

Geological map of the Cotswolds.

spherical grains (oooids) cemented together, each grain being formed of a central nucleus with layers of carbonate sediments around it. It is the finer-grained oolitic limestone that has been widely used in Cotswold architecture and for that reason is known as 'building freestone'.

The Inferior Oolite dominates the Cotswolds. The suite of rocks encompassed by this term represent differing conditions of deposition within the shallow Jurassic seas. Most of what is known as the Lower Inferior Oolite, for example, is made up of massive beds of oolitic limestones with a calcite cement in which large-scale bedding structures point to the build-up of banks of oooids: an environment comparable, in fact, with the clear shallow seas of the modern Bahamas. Evidence of small-scale current bedding in the Oolite represents ripples in the Jurassic sea. Fossils are not abundant in some rock types within the Inferior Oolite because the seas were shallow and subject to the intense wave action of 'high energy' depositional environments. But several layers in the Inferior Oolite, such as the charmingly named Pea Grit, formed from larger rounded carbonate algae growths known as pisoids, are highly fossiliferous.

The fossils, thicknesses, and characteristics of the Inferior Oolite reflect not only conditions at the time of deposition, but, additionally, reflect both the depth of the basin in which sediments were being laid down as well as later erosion and uplift. The much greater thickness of sediments in the Cheltenham-Cleeve Hill area, for example, is largely due to more rapid subsidence of the sea floor there with the material consistently filling in the deepening basin. On the basin edges, however, subsidence was slower and the succession of sediments thinner as a result.

Between the layers of the Inferior Oolite and the Great Oolite, itself a great variety of rock types, lies a thick layer of clay known as Fuller's Earth, the material once widely used in the Cotswolds for fulling (cleaning) wool. Fuller's Earth, known around Stroud (850050) as Stroud Clay, varies in thickness throughout the Cotswolds, being thicker to the south-west. The impermeability of this heavy bluish clay has in places influenced the position of settlement on spring lines, although as late as the mid-nineteenth century the practice of draining domestic water onto the Fuller's Earth frequently polluted wells and springs since the dirty water could not soak away and tended only to flow into public supplies.

The rocks making up the Great Oolite underlie parts of both scarp edge and eastern wolds, and, but for later erosion of the

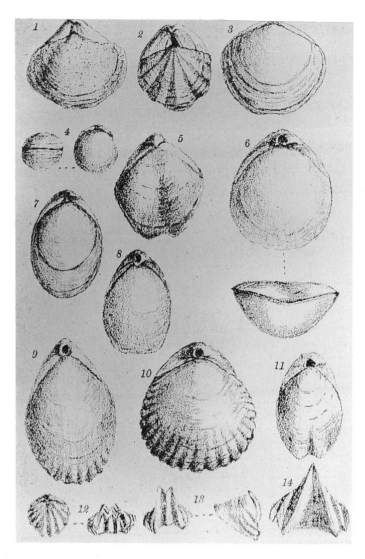

Some Cotswold fossils: 1 *Spiriferina rostrata* (Lower and Middle Lias); 2 *Spiriferina Walcotti* (Lower and Middle Lias); 3 *Waldheimia numismalis* (Middle Lias); 4 *Terebratula globulina* (enlarged: Middle Lias); 5 *Waldheimia resupinata* (Middle Lias); 6 *Terebratula simplex* (Upper Lias and Inferior Oolite); 7 *Terebratula punctata* (Marlstone); 8 *Terebratula sub-punctata* (Marlstone); 9 *Terebratula plicata* (Inferior Oolite); 10 *Terebratula fimbria* (Inferior Oolite); 11 *Terebratula globata* (Inferior Oolite); 12 *Rhynchonella variabilis* (Middle Lias); 13 *Rhynchonella cynocephala* (Cephalapod Bed/Cotteswold Sands); 14 *Rhynchonella acuta* (Middle Lias).

up-tilted western edge, would have covered all the Cotswolds today as once they did in the past. The principal sequences of clays, evenly-bedded limestones, and current-bedded shelly and oolitic limestones forming the Great Oolite reflect different depositional characteristics. The clays represent seas receiving muddy sediments. The limestones, especially those with oooids, represent perhaps more active but certainly cleaner conditions. Great Oolite freestone, sometimes called 'Bath freestone', has been quarried and mined for centuries. Many Oxford colleges are made of freestone taken from quarries at Taynton (235137), the source of the best building stone in the northern Cotswolds.

The rocks at the base of the Great Oolite are in places known as 'flaggy oolite', and, as the name suggests, are fissile and break into 'flags'. Because they easily fracture along lines of weakness and are used widely as roofing tiles, they are known as 'Cotswold slates', although they are not slates in the proper geological sense. The stone is cut in blocks and allowed to weather which, under the action of frost, renders the blocks capable of being split into thick layers. Around Stonesfield (394172), 'slate' quarrying in this way was once so widespread that the landscape is now pockmarked by quarry shafts, refuse tips, and hollows. In the east and south-east, the durable upper Great Oolite known as Forest Marble has also been long quarried and even used in sculpture. The rubbly shelly limestone known as the 'Cornbrash' is, however, not suitable for building. As the name suggests, the 'brashy' (broken, lumpy) soil derived from this rock is well suited to the cultivation of grain. In places, this shallow calcareous loam was known as 'stonebrash', and for some Cotswold farmers in the past, the size of stones and the local balance of clay and sand determined whether they planted corn (larger, hard stones) or turnips (in areas of small, soft stones).

The rocks of the Cotswolds have a variety of fossils. Roderick Murchison, the nineteenth-century geologist, writing in his 1834 *Outline of the Geology of Cheltenham*, noted that 'Rocks are to the geologist what *Papyri* are to the Antiquary, imparting to every one who diligently lays them open, the history of the ages that have preceded us'. Discovering the past Cotswolds through fossils is a pleasant way to spend a summer's afternoon and various guides exist for those wanting to identify fully what they've found. Quarries and exposed slopes are the best place to look, but take care at all times and seek permission for access to off-road sites. A nature trail in Chedworth Nature Reserve (053135) shows some of the species known from the Inferior Oolite and illustrates the environments in which these creatures would once have lived. Most of the brachiopod species of the *Terebratulid* and *Rhynchonellid* orders in the Chedworth exposure were suspension feeders, filtering minute organisms from the Jurassic seas; some are typical of clear marine environments; others suggest that brackish conditions also pertained.

Leckhampton Hill (950183) has several quarries in the Inferior Oolite and a number of the beds exposed are rich in fossils. South Quarry presents a good section of Lower Freestone and well-preserved brachiopods can be found in the screes to the foot of the rock face. At Top Quarry the top of the Upper Freestone, representing the highest bed of the Lower Inferior Oolite here, is overlain by the Lower Trigonia Grit. Above this is the Gryphite Grit, characterised here by the bivalve *Gryphea sublobata*, specimens of which may be found in the stones cleared from the fields on the top of Leckhampton Hill. One local name for them is 'Devil's toenails'. Elsewhere, ammonites and belemnites are abundant in the Lower Lias but less common in the Inferior and Great Oolite. Corals and sharks' teeth have been found, and in the Stonesfield Slate, remains of large creatures such as pterodactyls.

The fact that the Cotswolds today stand as a tilted 'layer cake' is the result of later uplift and tilting to about 2° to the south-east. But the rolling features of the Cotswold countryside are the result of changes in the more recent geological past. Some clay layers in particular, because overlaid by heavier rock strata, have been squeezed out and the heavy layers have slipped and slid downhill, or 'cambered' as it is properly known, to give the rounded edges of the contemporary scene. The present-day relief and particularly the differences between the steeper western scarp and the eastern wolds is also the consequence of drainage patterns. Of the principal rivers, only the Frome and the Avon in the south Cotswolds rise in the eastern wolds and cut across the scarp edge, at Stroud and Bath respectively.

Other rivers – the Dickler, the Windrush, the Coln, the Churn –
drain roughly north-west to south-east, and, on the gentle
eastward slopes, cut less deeply as they run their course. Where
small rivers and streams cut the scarp edge, they often incise
deeper into the underlying rock and have produced steep
valley sides as a result. Such faster-flowing waters, especially
where they run near deposits of Fuller's Earth, were important
influences upon the location of Cotswold cloth mills. The
streams in some valleys are now 'misfit', no longer carrying as
much water as in the colder wetter regimes during and at the
end of the Ice Age. Slad Valley (872073) is one such, 'slade'
being a Cotswold name for a hanging dry valley. The
Cotswolds were never glaciated but the melting of snow in the
warmer intervals between colder glacial periods may explain
why some larger Cotswolds valleys today have small water
courses.

There are several good vantage points on the scarp edge
from which to contrast the limestone scenery with the vales
beyond. Bredon Hill (960399), of Inferior Oolite, is the largest
of the Cotswold outliers and affords wonderful views of the
Vales of Evesham and Gloucester and of the Malverns to the
north-west. Moving south, Dover's Hill near Chipping
Campden (150390), Cleeve Hill (985266), Painswick Beacon
(868121), Stinchcombe Hill (740985), the scarp edge near the
Tyndale monument at North Nibley (746957), and the wolds
south of Cold Ashton (750726) all provide splendid vantage
points.

CHAPTER 2

Flora and Fauna

The type and distribution of Cotswold wildlife and plant life have been influenced both by the limestone rocks of the region and by the lie of the land with its characteristic scarp edges and gentler-sloping plateaux. Oolitic limestone has a very high proportion of calcium carbonate, a fact which affects the properties of the resulting soils, and, in turn, the type of vegetation. The Cotswolds are one of the best areas in the British Isles for 'calciphile' vegetation, plants tolerant of limey conditions. However scenically attractive it is as 'Wild Nature', the Cotswolds scene of woodland and scrub or downland is not a 'natural' vegetation in the proper botanical sense, but is 'semi-natural', being mainly made up of native species or naturally-introduced immigrant species.

The most common combination of tree species along the woodlands of the scarp edges is ash-oak-beech, with the last predominant. Between Birdlip (925143) and Dursley (752978) to the south, almost the whole scarp is beechwood. There are walks and footpaths signposted all along these scarp-edged beechwoods, but especially interesting botanically are the woods around Cranham (900130), which may be reached off the Cheltenham-Stroud Road (A46) or from a minor road off the B4070 south of Birdlip. This area was recognised to be of botanical importance in the 1940s during early identification, by the British Ecological Society and the 1945 Nature Reserves Investigation Committee, of what were later to become National Nature Reserves. Species to be found in Cranham Woods and in nearby woods include the Green Hellebore *Helleborus viridis*, the Hairy Violet *Viola hirta*, the Bird's-nest Orchid *Neottia nidus-avis*, and a whole range of rarer plants such as the Yellow Bird's-nest Orchid, *Monotropa hypophegea*. The range of flowering plants characteristic of the escarpment beechwood flora reflects the deep leaf litter layers of the woods and the low levels of light intensity reaching the ground.

On the downland and particularly on the steeper sides to the

13

many little valleys of the Cotswolds where the land has long been used for rough grazing, the typical vegetation is of grasses. Predominant species are Sheep's Fescue *Festuca Ovina*, Red Fescue *F. Rubra*, and other bent grasses, although the extent of these and other grassland species varies with the intensity of grazing. Since 1954, for example, when myxomatosis devastated the rabbit population of the Cotswolds, the coarser grasses such as Tor Grass have gained ground. Downland flora is best observed on the higher parts of the Cotswolds plateau: places like Cleeve Common (990258), Painswick Hill (870120), and the commons at Minchinhampton (855013) and Rodborough (850038) are good sites for a variety of orchids including the June-blooming Frog Orchid, *Coeloglossum viride* and Bee Orchid, *Ophrys apifera*, and species like the Musk Orchid, *Herminium monorchis*, which, although rare in Britain as a whole, is found quite commonly in some localities in the region.

In more sheltered spots, in abandoned quarries or where particular circumstances of soil and light permit, rare species such as the Pasque Flower *Pulsatilla vulgaris* or the Hound's Tongue *Cynoglossum officinale* may be found. But across the Cotswolds as a whole, there is much to delight the eye in even the commonest of plants, and many comparatively abundant or rarer species are ready to be discovered. On almost any walk, take a guide to flowering plants. This will tell you about plants rare and known to you like the several species of violet, the charming white and yellow-flowered Eyebrights, *Euphrasia spp.*, widespread along paths on Crickley Hill Country Park (933163), the striking blue flowers of the Viper's Bugloss *Echium vulgare* and the small blood-red flowers of the Scarlet Pimpernel, *Anagillis arvensis*. Observe, identify them if you can, but don't pick them. The removal of even a single plant, common or not, can destroy a season's reproduction for a particular plant community; the continued destruction of our plant life, apart from rendering the countryside colourless, has much more serious implications for the wildlife dependent in various ways upon it.

A wide variety of bird species is to be found in the region, both woodlands and downland, although numbers in different species vary greatly and their local distribution often reflects

THE RACK ISLE

THIS PROPERTY IS
HELD AS A WILDFOWL
RESERVE.
AVOID DAMAGING
NESTS OR EGGS OR
ENDANGERING YOUNG
BIRDS.

THERE IS A SMALL BREEDING
POPULATION OF MALLARD ON
THE RACK ISLE.
UNFORTUNATELY, FEEDING OF
DUCKS BY VISITORS HAS
ATTRACTED A DISPROPORTIONATE
NUMBER OF DRAKES. BECAUSE
OF THIS IMBALANCE, FIGHTING
BREAKS OUT RESULTING IN
THE INJURY OR SOMETIMES
DEATH OF SOME DUCKS WITH
AN ADVERSE EFFECT ON THE
BREEDING POPULATION. PLEASE
THEREFORE REFRAIN FROM
FEEDING SO THAT THE
NATURAL BALANCE MAY BE
RESTORED.
Thank you

The Rack Isle Wildfowl Reserve, Bibury (114067). The reserve takes its name from the area where cloth was 'racked' to dry after fulling or dyeing.

local ground cover and food source. Perhaps the most widespread of the woodland butterflies is the Speckled Wood but other species are to be found in that habitat and on the downland. Species of Skipper, the Meadow Brown and the attractively-patterned Marbled White all feed on various downland grasses whilst the much smaller Small Blue has Kidney Vetch as its principal food plant. Changes in land utilisation, particularly to downland since 1945, have very much affected the butterfly species. Both the Large Blue and the Adonis Blue have disappeared from the Cotswolds. Woodland moths such as the Leopard Moth and several kinds

of Hawkmoths are to be found in the area. For those with a
keener interest in small wildlife, there are several species of
snails including the largest British land snail, the so-called
Roman snail, from an erroneous belief that it was introduced
by the Romans. Near streams, the jewelled flight of Damsel-
flies may be seen. Dragonflies are not common. Britain's only
venomous snake, the Adder, is quite widespread in the
Cotswolds, but whilst notices warning about them are displayed
at places like Leckhampton Hill and Crickley Hill Country
Park, the snakes usually sense movement and move to safety
long before humans get near them.

The fox and the badger are quite numerous in the area, and
deer including the Fallow, the Roe and less-commonly the
Muntjac, may all be seen, especially in more heavily-wooded
habitats. The pulling-up of hedgerows and even their regular
cutting back by farmers and others have reduced the numbers
of creatures like the harvest mouse. Several species of bat are to
be found in the Cotswolds, but none is very common and they,
too, suffer as breeding places like old barns are knocked down
or converted.

Sharp eyesight and patience are needed to see the flora and
fauna of any place and the Cotswolds are no exception. In
addition to the more important beechwood sites like Cranham
and the almost limitless number of country walks on which at
least some interesting wildlife and plant life may be found,
there are, however, some sites where the looking is a little less
difficult. The North Meadow outside Cricklade (100935) is
famous for being the best habitat in the country of the rare
Snake's-Head Fritillary, *Fritilleria meleagris,* and the site is much
visited in early May when this lovely reddish-purple flower is
on show. For those interested in waterfowl, the Cotswold Water
Park near the village of South Cerney (055965) south of
Cirencester has attracted a number of interesting species
including the Great Crested Grebe. Near Bibury (115065),
there is a small wildfowl reserve called The Rack Isle. Bibury is
a popular place with visitors for many of whom feeding the
ducks there has become, as in many other places, popular
practice. Such feeding is now prohibited, however, as it has
attracted a disproportionate number of drakes. This, in turn,
has led to an adverse effect upon the breeding population:

Cotswold sheep, with their characteristic round and friendly face, graze with other breeds beneath trees in Stowell Park (088129), south west of Northleach.

another example, if less obvious, of the way humans unthinkingly alter the balance of Nature. But the best place to see wildfowl (though it is not within the Cotswolds proper) is the Wildfowl Trust Reserve at Slimbridge (740035), made famous by the late Sir Peter Scott. The Reserve is signposted from the M5 and the A38.

Interesting 'tamelife' in the form of rare breeds of farm animal, many of which nearly became extinct, may be visited at the Cotswold Farm Park (110269), just east of Temple Guiting, at Broadway Tower Country Park (113360), and at the Arlington Mill Cotswold Country Museum in Bibury. If you like your wildlife on a plate, the Bibury Trout Farm is a good place to choose a trout. The poultry at Folly Farm, a collection of rare breeds of domestic fowl situated off the A436 Cheltenham to Bourton-on-the-Water road about two miles from Bourton, number over seventy different species. Unlike Bibury trout, you can't choose your own. The most exotic collection of wildlife, the great part of it non-native, is to be found in the Cotswold Wildlife Park (242083), off the A361 south of Burford.

There are many gardens in the Cotswolds where it is possible

to discover a more managed flora than in the countryside itself.
Many of the finest gardens are mentioned in later chapters, but
particularly at Sezincote (175312) north of Stow-on-the Wold,
at the Batsford Arboretum (185337), and at the Westonbirt
Arboretum (855900) off the A433 south-west of Tetbury, the
range of the plants in the collections is as wonderful as their
setting is pleasing.

These gardens are the direct result of human activity in
creating a stylised nature. In their way such places, and the
woodlands and downlands which surround them, are the latest
form of that struggle between humans and the land that has
been taking place since the first humans settled in the
Cotswolds.

CHAPTER 3

The Peopling of the Cotswolds: from Prehistory to the Romans

In his *The Origin of Species* (1859), Charles Darwin noted that as a result of patchy fossil evidence for past lifeforms, 'The noble science of geology loses glory from the extreme imperfection of the record'. So, too, does archaeology. The evidence for former patterns of human occupancy, like the geologist's fossils, is not only restricted by the varying survival and discovery of artefacts but also by problems in interpretation.

In the Cotswolds, more is known of more recent periods of human prehistory than earlier ones, an understanding resulting almost entirely from the relative amount of useful and datable material that survives from, say, the Palaeolithic (very limited in the region) in comparison with the Iron Age (plentiful and widespread). It is a regrettable truth, too, that some of our knowledge of the past peopling of the area is despite, rather than because of, archaeologists. In the late nineteenth century, many field meetings of both the Cotteswolds Naturalists' Field Club begun in 1846 and the Bristol and Gloucester Archaeological Society established in 1876 would excavate a barrow or other site as part of their day's activities. The Bown Hill Long Barrow (823018) west of Woodchester was opened between 18th and 20th May 1863, for example, as part of the summer meeting of the Cotteswolds Naturalists' Field Club, and other sites at Notgrove and Cranham were similarly ill-treated. Such amateur work made later detailed interpretation doubly difficult, not least since this early digging seldom produced proper scientific reports. Whilst we know more now, we still seem not to know any better. Archaeological sites of great importance are being destroyed through arable cultivation and gravel extraction. Of the seventy Neolithic long barrows recorded in the whole of the Gloucestershire and Avon districts in the early 1980s, over half were then affected by ploughing. The situation has not improved in the last decade for these or other sites.

19

The earliest visible remains of human occupation in the Cotswolds are the Neolithic long barrows dating from 3500-1900 BC. But people have inhabited the area probably intermittently for as long as 250,000 years. The evidence for this Palaeolithic activity consists almost alone of stone and flint implements with the earliest recognisable objects being handaxes. The problem with handaxes is that whilst they have known variations around a shape that is triangular with a broad butt end and pointed tip, their basic efficiency meant they continued to be made and used throughout the Palaeolithic. Dating individual finds thus presents problems. Findspots for Palaeolithic implements in the Cotswolds include sites from the gravels in the Upper Thames Valley in places like South Cerney (050968), Meysey Hampton (120998), and Lechlade (217007). Other finds have been made at Great Witcombe (912147) and at Charlton Abbots (034242). Whilst there is no reason to doubt that Palaeolithic people were settled elsewhere and that they moved about within the Cotswolds, the few findspots and the fact, too, that even there handaxes are seldom found *in situ* means we cannot know for certain the patterns of human occupation over this extended period. Indeed, it is probable that continuous human occupation of the Cotswolds does not begin until post-glacial times and the Mesolithic.

At the end of the last glacial period about 10,000 years ago, climatic conditions began to improve and by c.6000 BC a warmer and wetter 'Atlantic-type' climate prevailed in the Cotswolds. The region offered rich natural resources and it is generally assumed that known Mesolithic artefacts now reflect occupation of the Cotswolds by peoples who were nomadic or semi-nomadic hunter-fisher-gatherers. The principal Mesolithic artefacts found in the region – usually (and paradoxically) found in fields where arable agriculture has turned up the flints – are 'microliths', small flints of a roughly triangular shape commonly used as arrowheads. Archaeologists use variations in the basic shape of microliths to date earlier and later phases in the Mesolithic. With what is known of Cotswolds evidence, Mesolithic occupation probably began relatively late in the post-glacial period.

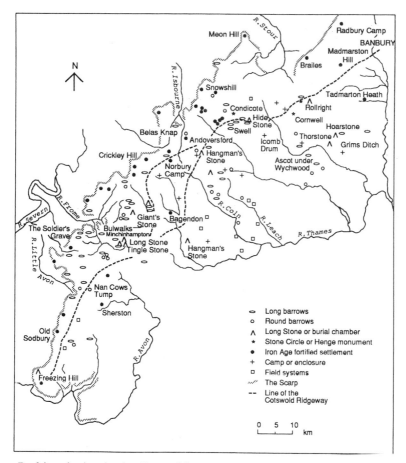

Prehistoric sites in the Cotswolds.

Important finds of Mesolithic microliths have been made at Syreford near Whittington (028204), a little north-west of Hazleton (073189), and in the south Cotswolds near Cherington (904986), and Long Newnton (910924), east of Tetbury. 'Important' in this sense means finds reaching double figures. But the fact that there are over thirty-five known sites across the Cotswolds, principally along the scarp edge, where just one or two microliths have been found, suggests a fairly densely-populated coverage by people able through use of fire and axe to clear the forest. Within this overall picture, some

sites were more important than others, even allowing for
differing amounts of fieldwork done. The Syreford site
represents a manufacturing settlement of some significance,
for example, and that near Hazleton has suggested to some
that the first, Mesolithic, clearance of the forest provided a site
in which Neolithic (and later) communities established
themselves. It would not be pushing the evidence too far to
suggest that Mesolithic peoples set in train that long process of
environmental transformation which has brought so many
culturally-induced changes to the Cotswolds.

Far more important in changing the natural landscape of the
area were the Neolithic peoples. They were the first farmers.
The Neolithic is dated on the basis of pottery types into three
periods: early, from c.3500BC to about 2900BC; middle,
c.2900BC-c.2400BC; and the later Neolithic from c.2400BC
to c.1900BC. Palaeobotanical evidence, principally the
identification of pollen grains from excavated long barrows,
suggests that the climate at about 3500BC was warmer if a
little wetter than in the Cotswolds now and that tree species
would be familiar to us today. The long barrow at Nympsfield,
for example (802003), has revealed evidence of ash, oak, hazel,
beech and elm as well as other species. Clearance of this
wooded cover was principally for grazing. Cattle are the
dominant species at the important settlement on Crickley Hill
(926162) and have also been found at the nearby site of The
Peak near Birdlip (923150). In some long barrows, the bones
of pigs, sheep and goats have been found as well as those of
dogs, cats and foxes. There is little evidence for any arable
agriculture, apart from poorly preserved carbonised wheat and
barley grains unearthed at The Peak and Crickley Hill, and
querns of Middle Neolithic date have been found at the latter
site.

Early Neolithic material is often found in association with
flints of Mesolithic age (as, for example, at Hazleton and also
on Cow Common near Swell in the north Cotswolds: (165263)).
The more plentiful evidence for the Middle Neolithic in the
Cotswolds reveals a distribution of sites of two main types:
enclosures (or causewayed camps as they are also termed), and
long barrows. A single unenclosed site is known from near
Gloucester, and near Lechlade aerial photography has revealed

a ring-shaped monument together with a twin line of banked ditches, of uncertain function. In addition to Crickley Hill and The Peak, causewayed enclosures are known at Icomb Hill (202232) south of Stow-on-the-Wold, near Eastleach Turville (198052), and at Down Ampney (100972). Crickley Hill has been the focus of prolonged excavation. The Neolithic site underwent several episodes of development with the earliest known enclosure being a double line of causewayed ditches, each of which has been filled and re-dug several times. Later enclosures would suggest that Crickley was a fortified village in the middle to late Neolithic: the presence of flint arrowheads lying in an entrance passageway and against the burnt stone palisade suggests an abrupt end to Neolithic occupation there. At Crickley and other causewayed sites, remains of pottery, ornaments, querns, bone implements, and flints as well as animal bones not only point to the subsistence practices of these early pastoral farmers, but, since the querns are of imported stone and flint is not native to the area either, they also suggest that these sites were the focus for systems of distribution and exchange within southern England.

The Neolithic long barrows of the Cotswolds have excited much attention now and in the past. The fact that they were burial mounds led some to believe they held buried treasure rather than human remains, and many long barrows have legends and folklore relating to coin hoards or golden coffins. In the eighteenth century, it was said of the Giant's Stone Barrow (918062) and of Money Tump (903048), both near Bisley, that 'men have had the terrifying experience of seeing headless human beings which have vanished' (as travellers approached). The truth is, as ever, less dramatic.

Neolithic long barrows represent the state-of-the-art means of disposing of the dead about 2900BC. Detailed excavation has revealed four main types in terms of the arrangement of internal chambers and entrances, but the basic shape is roughly trapezoidal or rectangular in plan with a horned entrance in front of which was a forecourt which possibly served a ceremonial function. Human remains are found in the chambers, the passageways and even in the entrances. But we cannot always be certain that numbers inferred from surviving bones represent actual population levels during the Neolithic.

Chambers may have been cleared out periodically – grave-robbing of tombs is known from the Roman period. And for reasons which are not altogether clear, these barrows were either deliberately walled-up or abandoned as funerary sites at just the period the settlement on Crickley Hill was razed. Other than claiming that such events represent a hiatus in peopling the Cotswolds, archaeologists are at a loss to explain them. Pottery types change – the characteristic late Neolithic 'grooved ware' has been found near Cam (758992) and Lechlade – but little is known in detail either of subsistence practices or burial arrangements. We do know that a 'henge' monument was erected near Condicote (154283), the only one of this type of monument that has been positively identified for the Cotswolds. But nothing is known of its purpose. Crickley Hill probably lay deserted for over a thousand years after the abandonment of the Neolithic site, but in other places along the scarp, the distribution of flints and other remains of the Neolithic in association with early Bronze Age material suggests some degree of settlement continuity when the first metal workers settled in the Cotswolds.

Based on pottery and metal artefacts, the Bronze Age is divided into three periods with the early phase beginning c.2000BC, a middle Bronze Age from about 1400-1000BC and the late Bronze Age ending c.650BC. As for earlier periods, the incoming of metalworking peoples is best thought of as an overlaying upon, rather than a replacement of, already established populations. In some places, Bronze Age round barrows are found in close proximity to earlier long barrows or even actually overlying Mesolithic material, and there is some evidence to suggest similar building techniques were used in long and round barrows, as at Burn Ground near Hampnett (100158).

From evidence in the Cotswolds and elsewhere in southern England, we know middle Bronze Age peoples were settled agriculturalists with established field systems, and, probably, organised and recognised territorial units. The existence of small homesteads has been inferred from ditches and storage pits found at several sites. Grave goods, principally metalwork, attest to the relative prosperity of these communities. Copper axes have been found at Hawling (063230) and near

Belas Knap Long Barrow (021254). Although this barrow is partially restored, the typical form of Neolithic long barrows is seen to good advantage in this aerial view (GX-12, Cambridge University Collection, copyright reserved).

Oddington (230259), but the richest assemblage has come from early Bronze Age barrows at Snowshill (093333). Late Bronze Age material is rare in the Cotswolds, but the discovery of what may be a late Bronze Age metalworker's tool-kit at Nottingham Hill (983285) within the walls of a known Iron Age hillfort has prompted speculation on the origins of these features.

Much more distinctly Bronze Age are the many round barrows found in the Cotswolds. Yet it is precisely these distinctive monuments that are at greatest risk from modern agricultural practices: a 1980 survey identified 215 sites in the Gloucestershire Cotswolds in comparison with the 340 sites recorded (for the county as a whole) twenty years before. The distribution of round barrows shows a marked concentration around the north Cotswolds, particularly around the Condicote area. This has been interpreted as a reflection of the relative

Using electronic techniques, archaeologists can trace the general outlines and plans of buildings before then planning any excavations.

degrees of social and political organisation throughout the region. But only one round barrow has been dated: that at Cow Common west of Stow, dated to c.1480BC.

The Cotswolds have two Bronze Age stone circles: at Cornwell east of Stow, and the more famous Rollright Stones on the northern fringes of the wolds (296310). The monuments here – the King's Men circle, the King Stone and the remains of a Bronze Age burial chamber known as the Whispering Knights – have inspired a great deal of legend and lore: dancing stones, stones that go down to the stream to drink when the clock strikes twelve, and stones that bleed if stabbed. Other Bronze Age standing stones have similar tales attached to them. Both the Tinglestone at Gatcombe near Avebury (882990), and the Longstone a little further north near Hampton Fields (887999), are said to run round the field when the clock strikes twelve.

Uley Bury hillfort (785987), one of the largest Iron Age hillforts in the Cotswolds. Traces of ridge and furrow field systems are evident in fields to the right in the picture (ARG-71, Cambridge University Collection, copyright reserved).

There is more fact though often no less myth associated with the Iron Age. Iron Age coins in the Cotswolds give names of specific individuals, like Bodvoc the Iron Age chief, said to have surrendered his tribe, the Dobunni, to the Romans in AD43. Properly speaking, the period begins in the Cotswolds with the limited use of iron-based metallurgical techniques by existing bronze-using communities, but most archaeologists point also to construction of hillforts as marking the start of the Iron Age. Older conventions divide the period into three: the Iron Age 'ABC' classification or the terms 'La Tene', 'Hallstadt' and 'Belgic' Iron Age are no longer used professionally. Current chronological dating, based on evidence from Wessex, divides the Iron Age into five broad periods: Earliest, Early, Middle, Late, Latest. The Earliest period covers the transitional phase from bronze- to iron-using techniques from c.800BC to 550BC, the Early from 500BC to c.400BC, with the Middle Iron

Age lasting until about 100BC. The Latest Iron Age is, in a sense, much the shortest in lasting from c.10AD to c.43AD, but although Britain was by then part of the Roman Empire, Iron Age practices continued beneath the Roman superstratum. The area has magnificent Iron Age hillforts. Most are situated on the western scarp edge in naturally defensive positions, though there are a few to the east and south. Eight of the twenty-six hillforts in the Cotswolds have been excavated: Crickley Hill, Leckhampton Hill, Nottingham Hill, Shenberrow (080334), Uley Bury (785987), The Ditches at North Cerney (012078), Norbury near Farmington (125155), and at Salmonsbury at Bourton-on-the-Water (173210). Crickley has had most attention. It is likely that the substantial stone-built and timber-laced rampart of Earliest Iron Age date here represents a defended hilltop settlement of some status in contrast to other less well-defended sites which may principally have served as enclosures for cattle. It is difficult when just standing in one of these hillforts to appreciate the feat of civil and military engineering they represent since the vertical drystone defensive walls are so ruinous and smoothed by time. Many hillforts were destroyed at or about 400BC, largely as a result of socio-political changes which left surviving sites dominant and with many-walled rather than single wall defences.

There are other types of Iron Age settlement in the Cotswolds. Near Lechlade, traces of round houses and field systems have been found and at Guiting Power (096248) the discovery of storage pits points to the existence of a small farm. There is an additional type of Iron Age settlement commonly termed 'dykes' although the term covers a variety of ditched and banked features. Two sites are significant in this category: Bagendon (017065) north of Cirencester, and on Minchinhampton Common (856013). Bagendon is, in fact, a complicated series of nine dykes whose relationship one to another has not proved easy to establish. There was an Iron Age mint here and the finding of coins of the Dobunni tribe together with Late Iron Age pottery and a sherd of early Roman ware for a long time suggested that Bagendon was the 'oppidum' or town of the Dobunni. Recent interpretations tend to caution on this point: as one authority notes, 'the concrete archaeological data known from Bagendon dyke complex are in inverse proportion to the amount of speculation about the site'. Much the same might be said about Minchinhampton, but if these two sites present uncertainties, the same is not true of the 'hillfort' at Salmonsbury. This site has thrown up evidence which not only points to a role as a trade centre on east-west commercial routes but also an established continuity of settlement from Middle Iron Age to the Romans. By the standards of their time, Salmonsbury, Bagendon and Minchinhampton were all important centres for the market exchange and distribution of goods of wide variety. Roman imports were known and probably prized as status symbols at least among the elite in the Cotswolds well before the Roman armies arrived in AD43.

CHAPTER 4

The Roman Cotswolds

For the simple reason that written accounts of the Roman conquest of the Cotswolds are both few and confusing, understanding the Roman influence in the region is, as for earlier periods, heavily reliant upon archaeological evidence. Much is known of some sites like Corinium (Roman Cirencester), and villas like Chedworth (054135) and Witcombe (902142) have an enduring attraction. But even professionals are cautious about the Roman Cotswolds: much is still to know. The area within the walls at Corinium, for example, has been estimated at 240 acres – six times the size of the settlement within the walls of the legionary fortress at Glevum (Gloucester). By the fourth century, Corinium was the capital of Britannia Prima and the second largest town of Roman Britain. Yet less than ten per cent has been archaeologically investigated and some of that was done quickly as rescue digs. And of villas especially, it is intriguing to consider that even the more substantial sites known are, in fact, records of the failed, or at least less-favourable sites, since successful villas have been built upon and now lie, beyond discovery, beneath the floors and walls of modern farms and towns.

The Romans conquered and garrisoned the west of England by about AD47. We know in several ways – from the desertion of the hillforts and the growth of more open settlements like the oppidum at Bagendon, in the development of wheel-thrown pottery and international trade – that the Iron Age peoples the Romans encountered were anyway undergoing change in the first century AD. The Dobunni had been increasingly subject to the political influence of their eastern neighbours, the Catuvellani, and coinage evidence suggests that the Dobunni had split into two kingdoms in the Cotswolds by the time the Romans arrived. Whether such a schism made Roman conquest of the region easier is hard to know, but what is known for certain is that the Cotswolds stood

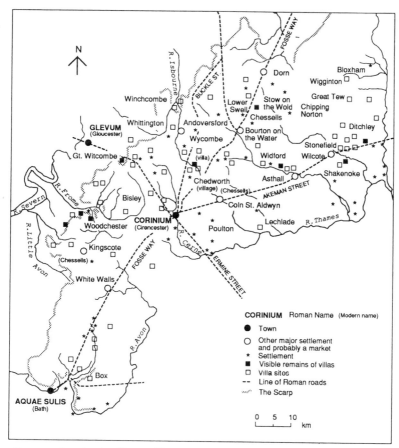

Roman sites in the Cotswolds.

as the western frontier of early Roman Britain. The frontier is clearly marked today by the line of the Fosse Way. Although modern roads depart in places from the line of this Roman military road – for example, at Jackaments Bottom (968977) near Kemble where the A433 swings west – there are sections like that on the A429 between Cirencester and Stow-on-the-Wold where the modern traveller follows directly a road designed to allow rapid deployment of troops 1900 years ago.

By AD52, the frontier had moved into the territory of the Silures in what is now south Wales, and by about AD78 the Roman conquest was effectively complete. The Romans now turned their hand to effective civil control. This meant urbanisation and the development of a rural economy based on market towns which were also centres of civil administration. In the Cotswolds, surviving evidence suggests that effective Romanisation of the region was concentrated on two main towns or *colonia*, Corinium and Glevum, together with several (known) larger rural settlements. Dorn (204340) just north of Moreton-in-Marsh, Bourton-on-the-Water (169207), Wycomb (024204) which is not named on modern maps but lies north of the junction of the A40 and A436 near Andoversford, and Lower Slaughter (165224) are, with Claydon Pike near Lechlade (215995) and Kingscote (819963), the most important of these Roman villages in the Cotswolds. Beneath these are the villas not all of which either had the same function or survive to the same degree. Yet – and if we may talk of a Roman settlement hierarchy – most people lived in small isolated dwellings at the bottom of the scale. The Romans brought new towns and villages and, for the elite at least, new standards of material wealth, but each was almost entirely dependent upon an agriculture and a countryside we still know little about.

A *coloni* was established at Glevum in about AD96-98 on the site of the earlier legionary fortress, and by the mid-second century it is likely that the built-up area had spread beyond the walls of this settlement. Roman Gloucester was an important civic and military centre in its own right, but it never enjoyed the status of its neighbour, Corinium. There is no unequivocal evidence to date the foundation of Roman Cirencester but the dating of several important civic centre buildings to between AD69 and AD96 is held to mark the city's beginnings. Such a date fits very well with the known withdrawal of the army from Dobunnian territory during the late seventiesAD.

The town was established north of the earlier fort. Like many Roman *coloniae*, Corinium was laid out in a grid-like pattern of *insulae*, perhaps thirty in all. Military engineers may well have helped in the early stages since it is thought that the first buildings closely resembled the legionary barracks. By the second century, however, stone buildings of high-quality masonry and interior fabric had replaced timber dwellings. In the central insulae were the forum and basilica which, together with the amphitheatre outside the town walls to the south-west, are the only known public structures in Corinium. The amphitheatre, which can still be visited, may at first have been a Roman quarry and the remains of quarrying are evident nearby. Perhaps as many as 7000 people could have been seated there. Its position outside the walls probably means that another theatre remains to be discovered somewhere in the town centre but neither it nor a baths has been found.

With public buildings came shops and private houses. Like their public and ceremonial counterparts, private dwellings appeared first in timber towards the end of the first century AD and then in stone. Several mosaics have been discovered in the houses subject to detailed excavation, the finest coming from a house in what was Insula XVII, now Dyer Street, showing Orpheus surrounded by birds. This mosaic has been dated to the fourth century and identified as belonging to what archaeologists refer to as the 'Corinian School' of paviours. Stylistic features of mosaic pavements in villas at Woodchester (839025), Chedworth, Witcombe, and Withington (032155) show that Corinian paviours were employed in embellishing the larger country houses in the Cotswolds, working, just as interior designers do today, from pattern books and in fashionable colours: Cotswold stone for whites and pale browns, stone from the Forest of Dean for the reds, Lias limestone from the vales for blues and greys.

Evidence gathered in the last decade or so suggests very strongly, however, that not all of Corinium within the walls was built up and that some buildings within the walls were farms. The plan of a house in modern Beeches Road has produced outlines of what has been interpreted as barns: excavators found an iron coulter from a plough and four bone weaving tablets which point to the processing of wool. Other parts of this substantial Roman city may also have been given over to market gardening: we just don't know given that the modern town overlies so much of the Roman one (in places to a depth of thirteen feet or more!). But the presence of this farm affirms the dependence of even the largest settlements upon produce from the land.

Much less is known about the larger rural settlements like Dorn, Wycomb, and those others mentioned above. The buildings at Kingscote would indicate that it was a substantial place covering perhaps seventy-five acres. It may have been a market centre in its own right. Like Lower Slaughter which has provided Roman material over an area of about twenty-five acres to suggest a temple but with little other firm evidence, Kingscote awaits further work. The Roman buildings on the Fosse Way at Bourton-on-the-Water were first uncovered during railway construction between 1875 and 1881 and have been examined on numerous occasions since. The remains of what are considered a posting house, a stable, and a bakehouse point to Roman Bourton being a staging post for travellers as well as a small market town. In contrast to Corinium, the settlement here was straggling and probably covered all that ground between the Roman Fosse Way and the nearby Iron Age site at Salmonsbury.

The small rural settlement at Dorn is the only one of these sites which was defended. Unusually for its small size (ten acres), Dorn had a regular gridiron layout to its streets. Both this, the evidence for walls, and its position only 200 yards west of the Fosse Way may mean it enjoyed military as well as local economic functions. In contrast, what is known of Wycomb suggests that it was a small roadside village of one main street with most houses having only one room. Yet there was probably a temple or at least some sort of site of ceremonial significance since finds include votive objects including a bronze statue of Mars. Like Bourton, Roman Wycomb was first discovered as the railway was being built at the end of last century and the embankment overlies several buildings. But the site in Black Close field and Wycomb field had long been known as a place where the plough turned up Roman remains. Fosbroke in his 1826 *Account of Cheltenham and its Vicinity* noted; 'In a field . . . called Wycombe or Wiccombe . . . coins from Nero to Valens have been collected in such quantities, that if rain has followed the process of harrowing, the country people go there to collect coins. Remains of black pottery have been found, and when the corn appears above ground, there is a discolouration, which shows that there had been a road or street all the way down the middle of the field'.

Field names and earlier names for places are an important clue to distribution of Roman sites, especially villas, in the Cotswolds. Modern 'Wycomb' comes from 'Wickham', itself

Great Witcombe Roman villa (902142) dates from about 250 AD.
Although only the first floor survives and has been partially restored,
it is likely that part of the building had a second storey.

stemming from *'Vicus'* (village) which shows recognition by
Saxons of a Roman settlement. The field name 'Stanborough',
for example, which derives from Old English meaning 'stone
fort', indicates that in the Saxon period and often for a long
time thereafter, substantial stone buildings from an earlier age
were still visible. The Roman villa at Frocester Court (789029)
is located in a field called 'Big Stanborough'. The several layers
of evidence here have revealed not only pre-Roman occupation
but have also suggested that the villa, first built in AD275 but
enlarged with a formal garden towards the end of the third
century, was probably not fully levelled from its ruinous state
until about 1300. The site was then under the plough until
1600 when it was laid to grass, and so it remained until
discovery in 1940. Elmstone Hardwicke (920260), a tiny village
north-west of Cheltenham, has a Villa Farm nearby, and an
extensive Roman settlement is indicated by the fourteen
'Stanborough' field names in the immediate area. The field
name 'Chessels' often indicates a Roman site, more often a
small group of roadside buildings than a single building. The

site at Lower Slaughter sits in a field known as Great Chessels and other examples are Kingscote and fields near the village of Coln St. Aldwyns (145052). Not all Roman sites reveal themselves in this way. The recent discovery of a small Romano-British settlement at Haymes near Cleeve Hill in a field called 'Wiremead' (976266) was the result of reservoir construction as well as land slippage on the hill slope. The villa at Witcombe was discovered by workmen uprooting an ash tree, and the extensive Roman remains at Barnsley Park in the central Cotswolds (080063) were only brought to light in 1941 when a dog had to be dug out of a rabbit hole there!

The term 'villa' is more complicated than it appears. If, as a simple definition, it may be understood as a stone-built domestic building in a rural setting whose chief function was as a focus for agricultural production, we should remember both that villas differed from farms as such in their degree of refinements including baths and mosaics and that not all villas would have been directly involved and to the same degree in the agricultural economy. Perhaps the villa in the Cotswolds may be thought of as the Roman equivalent of the eighteenth-century stately home or medieval manor farm: some were more luxurious than others, and though all were dependent on the land, proximity to towns and markets, soil type, and even the attitude of the owner to his labourers would all make for differences in the way such places operated.

Villas are known from all over the Cotswolds. Most of them belonged to or at least were run by natives rather than Romans themselves. There is no reason to expect these villas to be the same age and, indeed, they are not, but what is puzzling is the relative few in the Cotswolds which date from the late first and second centuries when the towns and larger rural settlements were expanding and the road system was established. The villas at Witcombe, Eastington near Northleach (129132), Chedworth, and at Cricklade (100935) and Box (822686) on the edges of our region can confidently be dated to before 200AD. But most other villas in the Cotswolds date from the last thirty years of the third century and later. One explanation for the differing chronology of foundation is that much of the area, certainly in the south Cotswolds, was managed as a series of great estates rather than run through smaller-scale concerns like villas. The later growth of villas has been attributed to the immigration from Gaul of landowners and agriculturalists fleeing barbarian attack between AD260 and 276. Developments in the form though not the function of individual villas sometimes reflect changes in the status of the occupiers. At Barnsley Park, the site before about AD360 had all the trappings of a small mixed farm of moderate wealth, but at or about that date and for reasons that are still uncertain, the existing timber dwelling was demolished and a substantial stone-built villa in the typical winged corridor style was erected. Even so, it is likely that this 'desirable residence with pleasing outlook in a sought-after part of the Empire' was occupied by a farm manager and not the landowner.

Barnsley Park is one of the few villas that has brought to light firm evidence on the agriculture of the Roman Cotswolds. The site, subject to intensive investigation between 1961 and 1979, has not only revealed ten phases of development between 140 and the fifth century AD, but also an almost complete arable field system from the Roman period. Of unique importance in England, the field system extended overall to about 250 acres but only a quarter of the area has actually been preserved after the Department of the Environment used their powers under the Ancient Monuments Act to halt its destruction under modern farming methods. That any of the field system survived until the late twentieth century is due in part to the land continuing in use within the same boundaries in Saxon times but chiefly because it was used as a deer park in the medieval period and thus remained almost undisturbed until it ceased to be used for this purpose in 1542.

Most villas were probably first and foremost corn farms though quite how good were the final products is open to debate: the contents of a corn drier excavated near Upton St Leonards (865148) included thirty-five different species of weeds as well as the wheat. But even in predominantly arable areas, livestock was grazed. Bones found at Barnsley Park indicate large numbers of cattle and sheep and increasing numbers of pigs in the later phases of occupation. The limestone uplands do not easily retain moisture even in wet periods and so are not suited to the grazing of large numbers of cattle which require a larger 'bite' off longer grass. But in the wetter soils of the south-east Cotswolds in the Upper Thames Valley, there is evidence to suggest a rural landscape of small peasant farmsteads and hamlets with principally pastoral agriculture. At the Romano-British sites of Claydon Pike and Roughground Farm between Fairford and Lechlade, wheat, barley and flax have all been found, but Claydon Pike especially seems to have been the centre of what has been described as a Romano-British cattle ranch. The Romanisation of the Cotswolds is best thought of as a gradual process. So, too, should the waning of Roman influence. We know that villas at Box (823684) and North Wraxall (838761) in the south Cotswolds were burnt in the second half of the fourth century probably following the large-scale raids by Picts, Scots, Saxons and Franks in AD367. Other villa sites not plundered reveal a downturn in material wealth during the late fourth century. Many, like Barnsley Park where the fields seem to have continued in use into the fifth or even sixth century, would have continued to provide for local and town markets. In Corinium, commerce was in serious decline by about AD430 since there seems to have been no money left to repair the forum. The evidence both of the silting-up of the cobbled roads in the town and of two unburied bodies is further proof of the collapse of civic authority by this period. As the town itself became decayed and perhaps depopulated, it is possible that the amphitheatre was occupied, for defensive reasons, as pottery and coinage from well into the fifth century have been found there. Wherever Corinians and others were living, a formal end to Roman influence probably came before AD577 when Cirencester, together with Bath and Gloucester, was captured by Saxons.

CHAPTER 5

From the Romans to Domesday Book

The Battle of Dyrham in 577 marks both an end and a new beginning to Saxon influence in the Cotswolds. Anglo-Saxon incomers took more than two hundred years to reach and conquer the west of England. The dating of several early cemeteries – Cirencester's Saxon cemetery dates from about 550 and there are other sites at Fairford and Bishop's Cleeve near Cheltenham – marks a gradual process of penetration ended in 577. This end to 'sub-Roman Britain' saw new beginnings in political administration since, by 628, the Cotswolds were under the rule of the Hwicce, a sub-kingdom of Mercia, and, to judge by the evidence of place names which incorporate Saxon personal name elements, many existing rural settlements were taken over by Anglo-Saxons in the seventh century. Gloucestershire first appears as an administrative division in about 1008 or perhaps between 900 and 980, and the short-lived shire of Winchcombe dates also from the early eleventh century. Much of our understanding of the political history and of changes in the Cotswolds' landscape comes from Saxon charters and the *Anglo-Saxon Chronicle*, and in the evidence of the Domesday Book of 1086 we have an unparalleled source to recreate the economy and wealth of the late Saxon Cotswolds.

It is unlikely that Cirencester, Gloucester or Bath was totally devastated in 577. Each town had been the centre of a kingdom before the Battle of Dyrham and earlier the centre of Roman territorial administration. A continued function as central places is suggested in the founding by Osric, ruler of the Hwicce, of monasteries at Bath in 676 and Gloucester in 681. Whether a monastery was founded at Cirencester in the short reign of the Mercian king Egbert (829-830) is uncertain. Archaeological evidence on the site of the nave of the Abbey has revealed a large Saxon church, built some time between the late seventh and ninth centuries, itself beneath a smaller church known to pre-date both the Conquest and the late twelfth-century Abbey. But it is doubtful if this was a monastic foundation. Other ministers were founded at Tetbury (890932) and Withington in the seventh century and at Malmesbury (933872), Bibury (115065), Hawkesbury (769869) and Winchcombe (025284) in the following century. Tetbury, Bibury and Withington did not survive the Saxon period though St Mary's at Bibury has a number of surviving Saxon architectural features as, to a greater or lesser degree, do a number of churches in the immediate radius of Cirencester: at Ampney Crucis (070016), Ampney St Peter (083013), Coln Rogers (087094), Cricklade (100935), Daglingworth (993050), Duntisbourne Abbots (971079), Duntisbourne Rouse (985061), Edgeworth (949060), Miserden (935089), Somerford Keynes (016956), and Winstone (966094). Beyond the Cotswolds' edge, a monastery was founded at Deerhurst (872296) in 804 – much of the original structure remains – and at Bradford-on-Avon on the southern fringes of the region, the chapel of St Lawrence, founded by St Aldhelm who was also first abbot at Malmesbury, is an important Saxon survival.

The founding of these monasteries and churches not only indicates increasing Christianisation and pacification of the Cotswolds but, since many monasteries in particular were the centres of large agricultural estates, also reflects a society able, organised, and willing enough to draw upon its agricultural surplus for their building. Both buildings and the rural economy of Saxon England were periodically disrupted by the incursions of the Danes. In 877 a Danish force retreating from defeat by Alfred in Wessex encamped at Gloucester and in 879 Danes spent a year in Cirencester. The *Anglo-Saxon Chronicle* records a series of such raids throughout England, some of the worst coming between 997 and 1016, and for the latter date it tells us that a raiding army '. . . went into Mercia, slaying and burning whatever was in their path, as is their custom, and procured provisions for themselves'. Raids and even the threat of attack would have made life uncomfortable for the farming population as well as inhabitants of towns and monasteries. For the Cotswolds in particular the fact that the region lay as a sort of buffer zone between the rival Saxon kingdoms of Mercia and Wessex made it difficult to present a united political front in the face of Danish attacks. One enduring result of later

This wall carving of Our Lord enthroned is one of three Late Saxon sculptures in the church of the Holy Rood, Daglingworth (993050).

Danish invasions was the parcelling-out of Saxon kingdoms and sub-kingdoms into manageable administrative regions. Thus were born Gloucestershire and the shire of Winchcombeshire, the latter centred on a defended town which, with its monastic foundation of 798 by Kenwulf, had for at least two centuries been one of the chief royal centres of the Hwicce. There is evidence of a 'Wincelcumbe scire' as early as 803, but however long the shire may have pre-dated its more certain origin in 1008, it was amalgamated with Gloucestershire less than twenty years later.

Certainly after the foundation of these Mercian shires and for some places well before, charter evidence documents the use the land was put to by Saxon farmers, and, indeed, it often records the changing character of the Cotswold landscape as trees were cleared and new settlements and farms established. The suffix 'ley' in Cotswold placenames derives from Old

English '*leah*', a clearing, and in several places, especially along the scarp edge, the species name of the tree is included as a further clue to the natural conditions facing Saxon farmers. Alderley (769909) south of Wotton-under-Edge comes from '*alor*' (alder) and '*leah*', for example, and Uley (788982) further north, which appears in Domesday Book in 1086 as 'Euuelege', the yew tree glade or clearing, is a derivation from the Old English '*iw*', the yew tree. On the western shoulder of the hill between Rodborough and Minchinhampton Commons stands the curiously-named St Chloe (845017). This first appears in a charter dating from between 716 and 743 as 'Sentodleag' and in 896 as 'Sengetlege', a clearing made by burning, from the Old English '*senged*' meaning singed or burnt.

Other names ending in '-ley' have an Anglo-Saxon personal name as prefix. Blockley (164350) in the north Cotswolds which appears as 'Bloccanleah' in 855 and 'Blochelei' in 1086 is 'Blocca's clearing', just as Barnsley is 'Beornmod's clearing'. Other placenames such as Yanworth (075138), 'lamb enclosure', or Sapperton (949032), 'soap-maker's farmstead', clearly suggest a specific function just as the name element '-ton' from Old English '*tun*', farmstead, suggests by its widespread coverage the extent to which small-scale agriculture was the basis of life in the Saxon Cotswolds.

We should not suppose, though, that appearance of a Saxon name element in a placename necessarily meant the wholesale replacement of the old order. A Saxon name need indicate nothing more than a new landlord. Several river names in the Cotswolds – Thames, Avon, Frome, Churn, Windrush, and Coln as well as the Severn – are British names. And at Nympsfield (802004), which appears in charter evidence of 862 as 'Nymdesfelda' and means 'the tract of open country belonging to a place called *Nymed*', a Celtic placename derived from British 'nimeto', a shrine or holy place, we have good if limited evidence for the probable more widespread survival of a Celtic-speaking population under Saxon lordship. It seems only sensible to suggest that a high degree of continuity of occupancy, if not also of economy, would exist among the smaller rural settlements of the Cotswolds. The village of Withington in particular has been subject to detailed scrutiny on this point and a convincing case has been made to suggest

Greenway Lane, running down the scarp west of Ullenwood (944168) follows the line of a Saxon droving road, used to drive sheep between estate lands at Brockworth (895164) near Gloucester and the high wolds at Upper Coberley (978158).

that the village, known as a Roman villa-estate in the fourth century, came through with its boundaries intact to become part of the Bishop of Worcester's lands during the late seventh century. The same boundaries persisted into the medieval period as Withington, whose name derives from *Widiandum*, the hill-pasture belonging to one Widia, grew in size and prosperity. It is possible, though by no means certain, that such settlement continuity characterised nearby places like Chedworth or Compton Abdale (063166), for example, since they bear Anglo-Saxon names yet were situated on or close to Romano-British sites.

As to the nature of rural settlements themselves and the type of agriculture practised, there is little beyond speculation. The several villages named Shipton in the Cotswolds provide one clue: 'Shipton' means precisely 'sheep farm'. There is documentary evidence to show that the monastic estates of Gloucester and Winchcombe were actively involved in large-scale sheep farming in the early eighth century and to show, too, that woollen cloths from the Cotswolds were being exported to the court of Charlemagne and elsewhere in Europe by the same period.

If little is known of the extent and productivity of pastoral farming beyond the fact that sheep grazing was important on ecclesiastical lands, almost nothing is known of arable farming. It is possible that the ridge and furrow features found in some Cotswold parishes today date from the Saxon period or even earlier. But the continued use of such features into the eighteenth century and beyond makes firm dating of their origin impossible. These features were formed by the plough turning the cut sod to one side only and the ploughman moving up and down the field to form, as the soil gathers in one direction, a series of ridges and hollows. On sloping ground, the effect of running the plough across the hillside is to turn material downhill. If ploughing continues so that soil is heaped up at regular intervals, then features known as 'strip lynchets' emerge as deposited soil becomes banks separated by almost level terraces. The Cotswolds' edge has nearly 100 'flights' of such lynchets, the great majority on the steep slopes between North Nibley (741958) and Bath (750650). Those at Coombe Hill (764940) near Wotton-under-Edge and at Hinton Hill (743765) are spectacular. Some lynchets are certainly medieval in origin, the result of bringing new land into productive use during periods of 'land hunger', but since Saxon charter evidence and placenames document extensive clearance not all of which can have been for sheep given the necessity for daily bread, it is possible that some lynchets are the remains of Saxon arable agriculture.

A much clearer picture of the late Saxon Cotswolds is presented in Domesday Book. Domesday was begun whilst William the Conqueror held court and 'deep speech' with advisers in Gloucester in December 1085. It is, essentially, a record of economic assets: who held land at the time of the 1066 Conquest, who holds it now and how much the land is worth. Information on the Cotswolds is contained within the

The late seventh-century Saxon chapel of St Lawrence in Bradford-on-Avon (825614) is one of the most important Saxon buildings in the country.

county of Gloucestershire. There are several omissions and difficulties with the evidence, not the least of which is the puzzling omission of records of downland pasture which makes it impossible to tell just how extensive and valuable were the sheep-runs at the time.

From what we are told, it appears that most of the 363 settlements mentioned in the Gloucestershire Domesday are to be found on the modern map. But not all Domesday names appear on the present-day map, since the village then has shrunk or even gone altogether to be remembered only in a farm name. Some Cotswold villages such as Randwick (830068), first mentioned in 1121, and Didbrook (054313) in 1269, do not appear in Domesday (although they may have existed then).

Gloucestershire had four boroughs in 1086, only Winchcombe being in the Cotswolds proper, the others being Gloucester, Tewkesbury and Bristol. The Cotswolds were well populated with most people living in small villages and directly from agriculture. It is interesting that the most heavily-wooded part of the area today was the same then. Woodland cover was thickest in two belts, in the north from about Winchcombe to Minchinhampton (860009) and, after a break, from near Wotton-under-Edge (758932) south past Chipping Sodbury (730820). On the wetter soils to the south-east, the proportion of meadowland recorded for some villages suggests more pastoral activity than on the higher wolds. Many valley and scarp-edge villages had mills. Some of these mills, which were mostly for corn, were old even then: there is a mill recorded in Notgrove (110200) in about 737-740.

We get a picture of a prosperous countryside. But it is also a picture of a dramatic, if quiet, revolution. Among the secular tenants-in-chief separately recorded, there is not one Old English name to be found. In the twenty years since Hastings, the Saxon aristocracy had been effectively replaced.

Take the example of the Domesday tenant of Hawling (064230), one 'Sigar de Cioches', sometimes also written 'Chocques'. Sigar, from the Pas de Calais, 'holds Hawling from the King. Countess Goda held it'. Sigar also held land in Hazleton (080181) and Yanworth as well as in three other counties. This entry is typical of so many across the Cotswolds. In this way, as Domesday recorded the end of the old aristocracy, so it also marked a new beginning.

CHAPTER 6

The Medieval and Early Modern Cotswolds

The Normans brought increasing economic prosperity to the Cotswolds and peace, too, although in several places remains of motte and bailey fortifications can still be seen – at Upper Slaughter (155232), Brimpsfield (941128) and Miserden (944093) in the north, at Newington Bagpath (816948), and at Ascot-under-Wychwood (299184) and Castle Combe (839779) to the east and south. With the exception of Beverston Castle (861940) west of Tetbury, castles have not survived well; those at Cirencester, Tetbury, and Chipping Norton are remembered only in local street names. Sudeley Castle (032278) near Winchcombe has buildings dating from the fifteenth century, but most buildings there are later. Beverston is an impressive ruin, the main survival a good example of a quadrangular keep of the early thirteenth century.

The prosperity of the early medieval Cotswolds is evident in the establishment of new towns and markets. The Domesday survey gives only two markets in the Cotswolds, at Cirencester and Bradford-on-Avon, although many other places would have acted as market centres without enjoying that formal status. Most new markets grew up along developing road networks. Northleach (114146) and Chipping Sodbury (734822) were amongst the earliest places to be granted markets, both in 1227, and grants of markets and fairs followed for most Cotswold towns in later decades: at Moreton-in-Marsh (208325) in 1241, for example, Wotton-under-Edge (755934) in 1252, a year later at Painswick (865096), and in 1269 at Minchinhampton (869008). Not all places so favoured benefited; the nearness of the markets at Cheltenham and Prestbury spoilt business and at Winchcombe, evidence from tax returns in 1187 suggests a decline in the economic standing of this former county capital relative to the newer towns. Most new towns of the Middle Ages had regular street plans comprising a single wide street from which ran long and narrow burgage strips. Northleach had about eighty burgage

47

freehold tenements by 1267, and at Chipping Campden there were seventy-six such burgage strips in addition to a number of cottages and lands held by less-privileged tenure. Later development has obscured this pattern in most places but in Northleach, Stow-on-the-Wold (199257), and most notably in Chipping Campden, the outline plan of the medieval town has survived remarkably well.

Outside the towns, most Cotsallers were both ploughmen and shepherds, any emphasis either way depending on local demand and, on the scarp edge and higher wolds particularly, on the availability of quality arable land. In this continuing balance between arable and pastoral agriculture, Cotswold rural life probably differed little in its material characteristics between the eleventh and fifteenth centuries and would have shared much in common even with today's farming. But in one important respect the medieval farming scene was totally different: it was open field agriculture with none of the hedges or stone walls we see today as field boundaries. On arable land, the simplest means of management was to divide the land into two fields, one to lie fallow with the other under crops, after which they alternated. This two-field system was well-established under the Saxons but, as population and demand grew, it became increasingly common on the more fertile vale and gravel soils to redivide the two fields into three. In any year, only a third and not a half of the arable now lay fallow. The main crop of many estates and farms was 'drage', a mixture of barley and oats, but a few farms even boasted vineyards and orchards. Stonehouse (808054) had a vineyard in 1086, and later ones are recorded in Bisley (904060) in 1324 and at Prinknash (880136). The Norman historian, William of Malmesbury (c.1095-1143), reckoned the product 'little inferiour in sweet verdure to the French wines' and wrote of the area as being then 'thick set with Vineyards'. He wrote also of 'Highwayes and Common Lanes clad with Apple trees and Peare trees; the ground of itselfe is so inclined to beare fruits, and these both in taste and beautie farre exceedinge others'. But the real riches of the medieval Cotswolds lay not in wines or fruit, but in sheep and their wool, both as raw product and finished cloth.

Wool was medieval England's greatest commercial asset.

The influence of medieval landholding patterns upon later urban development shows up well in this aerial view of Chipping Campden. The main street was built deliberately wide in the middle and narrow at the ends to accommodate large flocks of sheep at market (LD-31, Cambridge University Collection, copyright reserved).

That from the Cotswold flocks was noted for its depth and
whiteness of fleece though it was not as highly prized as the so-
called 'Lemster Ore' or 'March wool' from the Ryeland sheep
of the Welsh borders. The foundation of medieval sheep
farming and the wool trade in the Cotswolds was laid well
before 1086 but probably not until the late thirteenth century
did wool exports from this region and elsewhere in the West
Country begin to exceed in quality and quantity the output
from the east of England. Religious foundations like the
Cistercian abbeys of Kingswood (746919), Bruern (264203) and
Hailes (052299) had large flocks on holdings scattered across
the wolds. John de Gamages, Abbot of Gloucester between
1284 and 1306, is said to have increased the abbey flock to
10,000 sheep during his term of office. Even abbeys like
Westminster had Cotswold sheep runs, but although such
places had the largest flocks, the small flocks of the peasant
farmer totalled up to anything from four to seven times as
many sheep as the biggest monastic or seignorial landlords.
Adam Moleyns, author of the fifteenth-century *Libelle of
Englyshe Polycye*, wrote how Italian merchants 'In Cotteswolde
. . . ryde aboute', inspecting the flocks and purchasing the clip.
By 1341, Cirencester had ten wool merchants, most in regular
trade with Florentine, Flemish, and Genoese markets as well as
the domestic market, and the picture is repeated for smaller
towns.

From the second half of the fourteenth century, the export
of raw wool declined and was replaced by export of
manufactured cloth. High levels of production of raw wool
were still maintained, however. This proximity of the flocks to
centres of manufacture was one important reason for the
development of the cloth industry in the Cotswolds. Though
written in the mid-seventeenth century, Thomas Fuller's
comment on this advantage could apply two centuries before:
'whereas clothiers in some counties fetch their wool from far
off with great cost, it is here but the removing of it from the
backs of their sheep into their woolhouses'. There are other
reasons, natural and technical, to account for the development
of cloth manufacture in the region.

Of primary importance was the invention of the fulling mill.
Fulling is the process by which loose woven cloth is felted

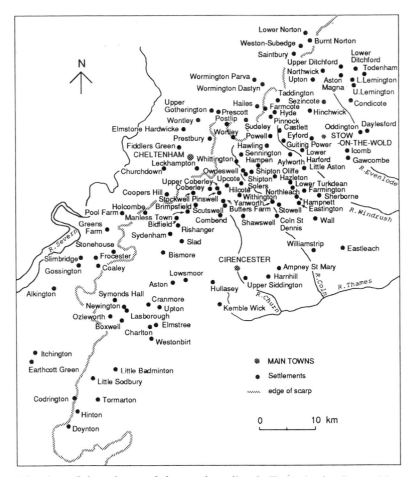

The sites of shrunken and deserted medieval villages in the Cotswolds.

together. Before the use of water-powered fulling mills, this had been done by drubbing by hand or walking on the cloth. The effect of this technical innovation was to shift the centres of production away from the towns, where neither the 'head' nor quality of water was usually sufficient to employ a mill wheel, to the countryside with its supplies of faster-flowing water. The numerous rivers and streams cutting through the Cotswolds scarp edge were ideal. Fuller's earth, used in cleaning the cloth, was available in deposits between the Great and Inferior Oolite, particularly around Stroud, Dursley and Minchinhampton. Teasels, used in raising the nap of cloth, grew on the clay soils of the vales. In the towns, restrictive guild regulations such as those which forbade weavers to send cloth to be finished (i.e., fulled) in the countryside, could not halt (and may positively have encouraged) the development of rural industry.

There is record of a fulling mill at Barton near Temple Guiting (094280) as early as 1185 – the earliest recorded one in England – but not really until the fifteenth century can we follow in detail the workings of the Cotswolds woollen industry. In one way or another, almost every town and village was involved. The principal product was a broadcloth, often called simply 'white broadcloth' but, since much cloth was woven without any colour and dyed and finished elsewhere, a more appropriate name would be 'undyed broadcloth'. Not all left the Cotswolds undyed. 'Stroudwater Scarlet', dyed with cochineal, was famous far and wide, and other coloured cloths to take their name from places included 'Minchinhampton Blue' and 'Uley Blue'. In the south, the scarlet cloths known as 'Castle Combe' took their name from the village where, from about 1410, the industry had been encouraged by one John Fastolfe, soldier, entrepreneur and later the model for Shakespeare's Falstaff.

The progress of the cloth industry was not untroubled. As early as 1418, we learn of theft of cloth from clothiers in Hawkesbury (769869) – a crime common in later centuries and punishable by transportation in the nineteenth century. And in 1485, the owner of the fulling mill at Chalford was attacked 'so that he was many times affrighted and disturbed, and was robbed of three Sherman Sherys (a type of cloth), worth 30s'. But the region received positive encouragement in the 1557 'Act touching the manufacture of woollen cloth' which, although it attempted to restrict textile manufacture to the towns in a despairing effort to protect guilds, excluded from legislation 'any towns or villages near the River Stroud in the county of Gloucester, where cloths have been made for twenty years past'. The industry received further stimulus with the immigration of Flemish weavers who brought refinements in technique as they settled in places like Wotton-under-Edge and

Bradford-on-Avon. The industry was organised on the domestic system in which the master clothier gave out his wool to be spun and woven in the cottages of the workmen. In some places the yarn was returned to the clothier before being put out again to weavers. After the cloth had been brought back, it was fulled and finished in a large mill, quite often the clothier's own property. The industry was dominated by these clothiers and wool merchants, early-modern commercial entrepreneurs to rival any of today's business tycoons. The rise of families like the Tames of Fairford, the Busshes, Forteys, and Midwinters of Northleach, the Willeys and the Grevills of Chipping Campden and other merchant-industrialists was one of the most important social accompaniments of the Cotswolds woollen industry.

Secular capital profited greatly following the dissolution of the monasteries. Monastic land sold to speculators by the Crown encouraged the growth of a gentry class in the area. With an eye on useful and vacant industrial space, some clothiers even erected looms in the deserted abbeys. In Malmesbury, William Stumpe bought the abbey and all its surrounding lands, outbuildings and immediate holdings for £1516 15s 2d in about 1542. The marks made on the abbey pillars by his looms can still be seen. And in Cirencester, John Leland reported how the abbey ruins housed 'a right goodly clothing mill'.

The legacy of the pre-factory Cotswolds woollen industry is partly evident in the weavers' cottages, mills, and workshops found throughout the region: at Arlington Row, Bibury, for example; along the Painswick stream; the Golden Valley at Chalford; in Nailsworth and everywhere in the Stroudwater area; and in the houses of the Tory and Newton in Bradford-on-Avon. More dramatically, the wealth created by the industry and the trade in raw wool is apparent in the magnificent later medieval 'wool' churches and in the manor houses of the gentry.

Amongst the most splendid of the Cotswold wool churches are the four churches of St. Peter and St. Paul's, Northleach, St. James' in Chipping Campden, St. Mary's Fairford, and St. John's in Cirencester. These, the jewels in the crown, are some of the Cotswolds' greatest glories, but the use of worldly wealth to fund sacred building has a long tradition in the region. The Norman doorways in the church at Windrush (193131), the *tympana* (decorated panels above the doorway) at Quenington (145042), South Cerney (050974), Ampney St Mary (075015) and Dowdeswell (001199), and the wonderfully decorated Norman fonts in the churches at Rendcomb (019097), Southrop (202034) and Hook Norton (355332) are all an enduring testimony to the skill of Cotswold masons and the close relations between the secular and the sacred. What distinguishes the later medieval period is not only the size and decoration of the churches in comparison with their earlier counterparts but the fact that it is possible to see, in the churches and especially in the houses, the development of a Cotswolds vernacular building tradition.

Not all the manor houses of the fifteenth and sixteenth centuries have survived equally well. North of Cheltenham, the west front of Southam de la Bere, built between 1512 and 1547 by Sir John Huddlestone, is now incorporated in the modern hotel. Early larger houses were usually either halls with a cross-wing or centred around a courtyard. The E-plan, characteristic of many Cotswold manor houses, probably first appears in the region in the 1576 re-working of Chavenage (872952). Horton Court (765860) dates from about 1521 although the north wing was built in the mid-twelfth century. Fine houses further south include the late fifteenth-century Great Chalfield Manor (861631). Both Horton Court and Great Chalfield are National Trust properties.

Later development and the nature of the original materials have meant that few houses of ordinary folk have survived intact or remain recognisably medieval. Good building timber was relatively scarce on the Cotswolds by the later medieval period but timber framing was widely used before then and for some later dwellings. Stone was used in conjunction with timber in most towns – although thatch, not 'slates' or tiles, was the common roofing material until the later eighteenth century. The finest surviving example of the technique employing timber walling set on ground-floor stone walls is 49 Castle Street, Cirencester, and the Bear Inn and the Fleece are other good examples in the town. What may be called the Cotswold style of stone-working and design – ball finials to the

Farmington (136154), with its former house and garden plots easily discernible in this aerial view, is a good example of a 'shrunken' medieval village (ANI-65, Cambridge University Collection, copyright reserved).

gables, mullioned windows with label mouldings – most widely
dates from 1570 onwards as the many towns and villages
rebuilt with the wealth from wool and cloth.
Not everybody shared in the prosperity of the medieval
Cotswolds. Indeed, one effect of the woollen industry was to tilt
the balance of Cotswold agriculture away from arable to
pastoral land: land under sheep was more profitable than
under the plough. In the late fifteenth century especially, the
open field arable of many Cotswold villages was enclosed and
put under grass. Some villages were totally deserted and are
now only bumps and hollows in the fields, but many more
shrank to leave only a church and a farm with remains of
house plots nearby. There are almost eighty sites of deserted or
shrunken medieval villages in the Cotswolds. Amongst those
with visible remains from the ground are Hawling (067231),
Shipton Solers (028185), Upper (199368) and Lower Ditchford
(228368) in the north, Farmington (137154), Hampnett
(100159), and Whittington (014210).
It is possible that these and other places were deserted for
reasons other than enclosure of arable land for pasture. Tax
lists of 1327 for the now-vanished village of Little Aston in
Cold Aston parish (129198) show increasing population, yet
pottery and other evidence suggest a complete desertion by the
middle years of the fourteenth century. This cannot be
attributed to the ravages of plague, the Black Death of 1348-
1349, as used to be thought in explaining village desertion
since Little Aston and others like it were in decline before then.
Desertion stemmed from a conjunction of poor climate, and
continued loss on returns per acre of grain as well as
population decline. The presence of these former villages is a
reminder that the Cotswolds landscape is a flexible thing,
always older than we think and always changing.
By the early seventeenth century, the distribution of towns
and villages was much as we know it now (although Sezincote
village (173309) was not enclosed and deserted until 1638).
From John Smyth's 1608 survey *Men and Armour for
Gloucestershire*, we get a picture of the occupations of men
between 20 and 60 years old in the towns. The textile industry
dominated non-agricultural employment. Painswick, for
example, had thirty-three weavers, four clothiers, and ten

This building, opposite St Peter's in Winchcombe (025282) and known simply as the 'Jacobean House', shows a number of the architectural features typical of the Cotswold style in the seventeenth century: gables with ball finials, mullioned and transomed windows.

tuckers. Bisley in 1608 had six fulling mills, four dye houses, and fourteen rack rooms, and twenty-nine of its 106 tenants held 'watercourse', rights to water needed in the manufacture of cloth. Half the men in this age range were employed in agriculture: on the wolds, sheep dominated and in the vales cattle. Along the scarp edge, Cotswold water had much the same concentrating effect on the location of industry as coalfields were to have in the nineteenth century: as Smyth charmingly observed: 'Many hundreds, even thousands, of springs breake forth at the sydes, knees and feete of those hills, begettinge divers delicate small rivers, neither knowing want of water in sommer nor so increasinge their chanell in winter, that the trade of clothinge, which heere aboundeth, is neither in drought nor wet wether hindred'.

Cotswold life was hindered in the seventeenth century, however, both by a downturn in the 'white' cloth trade and by the Civil War. The Thirty Years' War, begun in 1617, and an earlier misconceived attempt to undertake finishing of cloths before export, undermined clothiers' profits and reduced many workers to poverty. In 1621, weavers, spinners, and fullers were all complaining of the lack of work 'and, consequentlie, of means of reliefe for themselves and their families'. One petition of 1633 was drawn up in Kings Stanley (812036) and Leonard Stanley (802036) by 800 persons 'hitherto employed in clothing, and now likely never to be employed again'. The industry had largely recovered by the early 1640s, chiefly through moving from predominance in undyed cloth to manufacture of dyed 'medleys' or 'Spanish cloths' using Spanish merino wool, when the Civil War began.

The Cotswolds was vital strategic territory in the Civil War. Royalist support centred in Wales, the south-west counties and in the King's headquarters of Oxford was separated by Parliamentary forces in Gloucester and Bristol, the smaller towns of Cirencester and Malmesbury and by a good deal of anti-royal sentiment amongst clothiers and textile workers. Battles at Edge Hill just beyond the Cotswolds north edge in 1642 and at Stow-on-the-Wold in 1646 effectively demarcate the war as a whole, but the region saw a great deal of fighting in the interim. Cirencester fell to a Royalist siege in 1643. Malmesbury changed hands four times between February and May that year. Lansdown Hill, near Bath, saw heavy Royalist losses in 1643. The scars of the war are evident today: bullet holes in the abbey church at Malmesbury and Painswick; the *graffiti* of prisoners in Painswick and Burford churches; in Chipping Campden, the ruins of Campden House burnt by Prince Rupert's troops in 1645 to stop Parliamentary forces occupying it.

Both daily life and landscape recovered quite quickly. By 1677, Cotswold weavers were being sought by London companies to develop textiles in Ireland. The 1660s saw a return to that high level of building which had typified the years before the Civil War: amongst the larger country houses, both Badminton (805826) and Dyrham Park (742758) underwent rebuilding from this period. Others followed in the wake of the most important family of Cotswold masons, the Strongs of Taynton and Barrington, in whose works it is possible to see the merging of local vernacular traditions with more widely-practised designs. Only around Winchcombe did poverty continue. The tobacco industry there, begun about 1621, was prohibited by Parliament in 1653 as a threat to English interests in the West Indies. Dragoons rooted out the crops in 1667, but not until the 1690s did this local industry finally cease.

CHAPTER 7

Cotswold Life in the Eighteenth and Nineteenth Centuries

For all that goods and people had been moving in and out of the Cotswolds for hundreds of years, travel in the region by 1700 was neither easy nor quick. As late as 1807, Thomas Rudge, writing in his *General View of the Agriculture of the County of Gloucester* how 'The badness of the roads was for many years a great check to the industry of the farmers of this county', called for better roads as a means to agricultural improvement. Rudge's observation is echoed by other earlier commentators (and some later ones, too). What makes Rudge's comment so telling is that the eighteenth century had seen major expansion in the road network across the Cotswolds.

Important roads from earlier periods – the prehistoric Jurassic Way, Roman roads, or the medieval saltways – were not always suited to later needs. What distinguished development from the eighteenth century was the growth of toll or turnpike roads: a system which charged users a toll, and, theoretically anyway, drew sufficient funds from travellers for each parish to maintain its stretch of road. The first toll road in the area was from Gloucester to Birdlip in 1698. Market towns nearer the scarp had turnpike roads earlier than those in the wolds. Dursley and Wotton-under-Edge had a connecting toll road in 1726, Painswick had one with Gloucester in 1733. By 1743, the road between Bath and Cirencester (the present A46 and A433) was turnpiked and Cirencester to Moreton-in-Marsh via Northleach and Stow-on-the-Wold (the A449) followed in 1751. That year saw the turnpiking of the Oxford to Northleach road (the A40). The most westerly section of this road on the wolds, as it passes north of Andoversford and past Whittington and Dowdeswell (002198) to Cheltenham, dates from 1807: an earlier turnpike of 1756 had taken travellers, often at breakneck speed, down the steeper descent at Dowdeswell. Further south, the Nailsworth Valley Trust, formed in 1780, constructed what is now the A46 between Nailsworth and Stroud and the A434 from Nailsworth to

Sheep-shearers at work near Chipping Campden, c.1900.

Avening (883979) and Tetbury.

As well as goods, these roads brought a great deal of coach traffic, especially to places like Burford and Tetbury. In 1780, it took sixteen hours to reach Cirencester from Minchinhampton travelling on the 'Hampton and Cirencester Machine'! Unimportant places now like Hyde (886015) and Upper Hyde or Burnt Ash (887012) east of Minchinhampton were then staging posts as well as collecting points for carriers of goods. Cheltenham, prospering with travellers to its spas, had regular daily coaches to Oxford, London, Birmingham, Shrewsbury and Holyhead as well as to the other spas of Leamington and Malvern.

Canals were more limited in extent and purpose. There had been schemes to make the Stroudwater navigable between Stroud and the Severn as early as 1697, but not until 1776 was the Stroudwater Navigation begun. The eight miles and twelve locks between Framilode on the Severn (752102) and Wallbridge near Stroud took three years to complete. It was built to bring in coal from Shropshire, Staffordshire, and the Forest of Dean and take out the woollen products of an industry increasingly concentrating in the Stroudwater area in mills and factories. In part, the Stroudwater Navigation followed the line of the Kemmett Canal, built from 1759 to 1763, which connected Framilode with Stonehouse (805055). What really made the Stroudwater Navigation effective was its eastern extension, the Thames and Severn Canal, built between Stroud and Lechlade from 1783 to 1789. On completion of the Thames and Severn Canal on November 19th 1789, contemporary newspapers noted how 'This day was effected the greatest object of internal navigation in this kingdom. The Severn was united to the Thames . . .'

Before railways, both companies prospered well enough with the transport of coal, cloths, and other goods but dividends to investors were never high: on the Stroudwater system, they dropped from nearly 23 per cent in 1844 to 5 per cent by 1880. Built on porous limestones, the Thames and Severn Canal was plagued by problems of sufficient water, especially on the higher sections between Coates (980010) and Siddington (035995). Costs of leakage and compensation paid to local millers reduced profits well before the effects of the Great Western railway line from Swindon to Gloucester up the Golden Valley opened in 1845. The Thames and Severn was finally closed in 1933 and the Stroudwater canal in 1954, the last toll having been paid in 1941. Despite subsequent neglect, there is still much to see: classical portals at the Coates end of the Sapperton tunnel; old locks near Brimscombe Port, the former focal point of the Thames and Severn system; and lovely towpath walks east from Chalford.

For reasons both financial and geological, the Cotswolds proved resistant to the development of an efficient railway system despite the 'railway mania' of the nineteenth century. Few towns today are well-served by rail in comparison with a century ago, but even when the network was at its most extensive, few of the later lines paid. Places which had previously depended on the passage of goods and people – Northleach, Burford, and Marshfield (782738) most particularly – never had a railway link and went into serious decline in consequence.

The first Cotswold railway was a tramway laid from Leckhampton quarries in 1798 by Charles Brandon Tyre. From 1811, this system for removing building stone was extended as the Gloucester and Cheltenham Tramroad and for fifty years carried stone direct from the hill by horse-drawn tram to Gloucester. (In Cheltenham, the modern line of Andover Road and Norwood Road north of the junction with the Bath Road and Leckhampton Road follows the tramway route.)

The relative difficulties involved in crossing the western scarp meant that steam railways entered the Cotswolds first from the south in the form of the Great Western, and, later, from the north in the form of that line of the Oxford, Worcester, and Wolverhampton railway, opened in 1853, which followed the Evenlode Valley. The Great Western line was completed in 1841: the west end of Box Tunnel (830689) – reckoned by contemporaries 'monstrous and extraordinary, most dangerous and impractical' – shows well the difficulties faced by Brunel and other engineers. A branch line northwards via Kemble and Cirencester – the Cheltenham and Great Western Union (later absorbed by the GWR) – brought the railway to Cheltenham in 1847.

One of the effects of railway expansion, in the Cotswolds as elsewhere, was the regulation of time. Not all railway companies operated by 'London time', the moment the sun was directly overhead in Greenwich. As the sun moved west, so noon varied. There was a time when Victorian travellers could obtain watches with two or more dials to show local time and 'London time'. The Great Western was the last major company to adopt 'London time', in 1852; in Stroud (and Bristol) this abolition of local time was the cause of demonstrations against the 'imposition of London'.

However much improved communications brought major if unequal changes in Cotswold life well before the motor car, the major change in this period was to the landscape itself – in the form of parliamentary enclosure of the open fields. Sheep farming, in association with arable fields of fodder and grain, was predominant on the wolds by 1700 as it had been for centuries before. But open fields could not easily respond to increased demand and innovations in farming. Given the absence of field boundaries, the whole of each field was of necessity under the same crop. But the scattered nature of individual holdings of narrow strips was wasteful. Small-holdings managed this way required more effort than if they were brought together as part of regular field systems in which livestock could be easily tended, fodder crops such as turnips grown as winter feed and detached strips re-allocated as compact blocks. The stone walls and regular geometry resulting from these changes are everywhere apparent in the Cotswolds: today's rural tranquillity masks a major process of change begun first in Farmington in 1713 and ending with the extinction of common rights to Sodbury Commons in 1908 and of open field strips at Elmstone Hardwicke in 1914.

William Marshall records in his 1796 *Rural Economy of Gloucestershire* that the Cotswolds 'lay almost entirely in an open state' until the middle of the eighteenth century. Some parishes had been enclosed by 1517 but parliamentary enclosure differed from these enclosures by agreement in being a process which overturned by law existing customary rights. Although strung out over two centuries, the majority of enclosure Acts in the Cotswolds were passed in two 'bursts' of dramatic change: 47 Acts between 1760 and 1784 and a further 81 between 1793 and 1825.

In the vales, quickset hedges and post and rail fences were used to enclose the fields, but on the Cotswolds the abundant local stone was used. In 1807, 'walling on the wolds, 4'8" high, covered at top with broad stones, without mortar' cost 8s a yard. Day wages for a male labourer were '1s 6d with drink' (winter rate), 2s in summer, and always less for women. Rudge noted that Cotswold wage rates were often '. . . something less, and not so great an allowance of drink' as in the vales. The yearly wage of a headman was between £8 and £12, that of an undermaid no higher than £5.

Enclosure brought increased production of corn and meat and allowed the development of 'seven-field husbandry', a rotation cycle variously involving turnips, barley with seeds, sheep, mown seeds, vetches and peas, and oats frequently with sainfoin. Rudge reckoned to encourage population, too: 'To obtain corn from waste lands, and not to obtain people from the corn, is to rest satisfied with the means without the end'. But to judge from parishes like Aston Subedge (137415) whose population declined from 104 following enclosure in 1771 to 63 in 1779 when Rudder wrote his *New History of Gloucestershire*, the effect of enclosure on the labouring poor and smallholder class was not always beneficial. In 1733, a bill for enclosing the commons and wastes of Bisley was rejected following petition from the labourers and freeholders. In Minchinhampton, manorial customs had allowed weavers to enclose a portion of the commons since the fourteenth century. It is likely that the same applied to Bisley where we learn in 1733 of 800 dwellings and smallholdings scattered across the open Bisley Commons, each plot the property of 'Carders, Spinners, Weavers, and numberless Artificers' employed in the domestic branches of the woollen industry. These small plots, each with their few chickens and perhaps a cow or two, provided an important means of support to weavers' families during downturns in trade and there was bitter complaint when Bisley Commons were enclosed in 1869.

Country life was heavily dependent on the quality of harvest and upon the price of bread in relation to wages. In 1801, the harvest was exceptional: at Brimpsfield the crops were said 'to have exceeded in quality as well as in quantity any former year in the memory of the oldest liver'. But prices were high and crowds stopped out-movement of grain through Tewkesbury, Burford, Kingswood and Stroud in riotous disturbances in 1795 and in 1801. Riots were widespread in the Forest of Dean during these two years. On 8th March 1801, campaigners in Painswick for a 'just price' to a loaf set fire to a hayrick near the town. By the later 1820s and throughout the 1830s, falls in wages, enclosure, and advances in mechanised farming deepened the poverty of the Cotswold agricultural labourer. In November 1830, that wave of riots and arson known as 'Swing Riots' (after a 'Captain Swing' whose name appeared on threatening letters to landlords buying new machinery), first surfaced in the Cotswolds in Tetbury, having spread along the coaching routes from south-east England. The Tetbury affair, in which an automated threshing machine was set alight, was followed by similar incidents at Chavenage, Fairford, Bibury, Quenington, Coln Rogers (085094), Coln St Aldwyns (145053), Horsley (840980), Eastleach Turville (198053), and Southrop (201035). In Winchcombe and in Dumbleton and Deerhurst in the Vale of Evesham, ricks and barns were set ablaze. These outbreaks caused much alarm among the landowning classes. Of the 169 prisoners brought before Gloucester Quarter

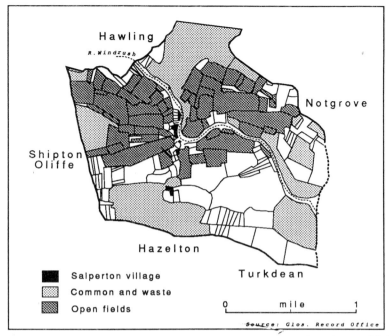

Hawling

R. Windrush

Notgrove

Shipton
Oliffe

Hazelton

Turkdean

■ Salperton village
▓ Common and waste
▒ Open fields

0   mile   1

Source: Glos. Record Office

The effects of parliamentary enclosure upon the Cotswolds'
agricultural landscape may be seen by comparing these two maps.
Salperton in 1741 was in open-field agriculture with individual
holdings scattered widely.

Sessions on 4th January 1831, 86 were charged with machine
breaking and rioting: only five were acquitted. Twenty-four
men were transported to Van Diemen's Land (Tasmania),
landing there on 31st May 1831.

Such protests against poverty were untypical of the
agricultural scene but they illustrate the feelings of a few at
the way traditional sheep-corn husbandry was maintained with
fewer and fewer labourers during the nineteenth century. One
commentator, writing in 1854 of Cotswold agriculture,
considered 'the present tenant farmer, in point of education,
social standing and real intelligence, to be far superior to the
past generation of farmers'. So perhaps they may have been,
and agricultural societies like the Kingscote Farmers' Club, the
Cirencester and Gloucester Agricultural Association, and the
Cirencester and Fairford Farmers' Club were no doubt

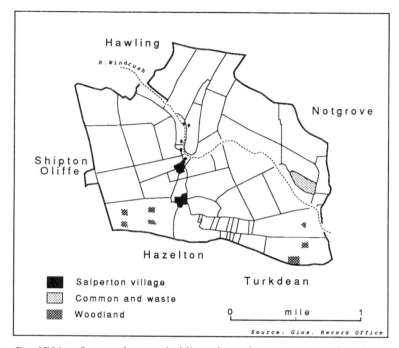

Hawling

R. Windrush

Notgrove

Shipton Oliffe

Hazelton

Turkdean

Salperton village
Common and waste
Woodland

0   mile   1

Source: Glos. Record Office

By 1781, after enclosure, holdings have been aggregated and new field boundaries have appeared, based only in part upon earlier divisions.

influential. So, too, was the Royal Agricultural College at Cirencester, founded in 1845 and still very important in promoting scientific agriculture. But present generations tend always to disparage the 'immemorial customs' of past generations. Farm life in the 1800s was good for those in full employment, often uncertain for the daily or seasonally-employed hand. Not until 1872 were farm labourers in the Cotswolds active in trades unions, and neither labourer nor landlord did well during those agricultural depressions in the later nineteenth century which followed widespread poor harvests and large-scale outbreaks of disease amongst livestock.

Cotswold life long recognised a distinction between agricultural society and those folk who lived in the countryside but, although they had a smallholding, were chiefly employed in textiles. This relationship took time to change. Mr W. A. Miles who headed the 1839 Hand Loom Weavers' Commission of Enquiry in Gloucestershire considered the continuation of the allotment system in the weaving districts to have a moral purpose: 'it gave the individual weaver a stake in the hedge . . . kept them as a group away from the beershops and behind their interests in the welfare of the community'. Some weavers were still employed in the domestic system and had a small plot in the early 1900s. But the appearance of the factory hand increasingly if not alone dependent on wage labour was an important change in the means of livelihood in the clothing districts.

In his 1712 *Ancient and Present State of Glocestershire,* Sir Robert Atkyns (whose splendid effigy lies in Sapperton church) reckoned the clothing trade so predominant that 'no other deserves a mention'. So it continued for much of the eighteenth century. But by the mid-nineteenth century, many mills had been converted to alternative uses and textile employment was much reduced. When, in 1833, Factory Commissioners visited Wotton-under-Edge, Uley, and Dursley, they found 12 of 19 manufacturers had ceased production within the previous three years. A further 1000 people lost their jobs when Sheppard's of Uley closed in 1837. By 1861, only 6,716 persons were employed in the woollen industry in the whole of Gloucestershire, a figure which fell to 3,898 by 1901.

The reasons for these changes are many and involved. Declining profits from export after about 1720 stemmed not only from foreign and domestic competition (principally from Yorkshire) but from belief among some buyers that Cotswold wool had degenerated in quality. This was not as bad in fact as critics imagined but it is true that Cotswold wool was not spun as fine as some others. Failure to maintain a system of wage regulation led to a petition in 1756 complaining of 'The great hardships which the Weavers thus groan under and the Extream poverty to which many of them are reduced', and the downturn in trade was such that even clothiers of the status of Daniel Packer of Painswick thought in 1768 of quitting manufacture altogether.

The industry recovered, as it had done before, by making more of what sold — fine cassimeres, fancy cloths, and flannels — but a severe depression in trade followed the hard winter of

The employees and directors of the Chalford Stick Company Ltd., outside St Mary's Mills, c.1910.

1783: the *Gloucester Journal* reckoned there were 15,000 destitute persons in the Stroudwater clothing parishes by early 1784. Small independent clothiers and manufacturers began to disappear in times of decline, partly from bankruptcy but also because they could not adopt the new machinery and accommodate both workers and machines in purpose-built buildings powered by water and coal. There were spinning machines in mills at Ebley and Dursley by 1788, and the introduction of scribbling machines (scribbling is the process of drawing out the wool fibres before spinning) caused riots in Woodchester amongst those whose craft was threatened. Power looms were not adopted in large numbers until the 1850s, and by then the handloom weavers were much depressed as an artisan class.

The principal causes of their depression were the introduction of unapprenticed labour, common during the Napoleonic Wars as the industry recovered to meet army demand, and decline in wages. There had been unrest about the use of unapprenticed labour in Uley in the 1790s, but worse was to follow in the 1825 strike. The three-month strike by weavers which began on 28th April 1825 was not unique to the Cotswolds woollen industry:

there had been other strikes, in 1726, 1739, and 1755. But what underlay the events of 1825 was a resolution by the skilled handloom weaver to protect his skilled status and fight for a living wage. Meetings and marches by weavers and others were held throughout the Stroudwater district in May and June 1825. At first weavers took action, almost reluctantly in the case of some, against fellow weavers to ensure solidarity: we learn how 'On June 4th, a "mob" went to a man named Burford aged 80, and expressing the utmost concern for the unavoidable necessity they were under of visiting him with their vengeance, they ducked him but without violence'. Shuttles were hidden, often in church towers, to ensure compliance. Ducking millowners in their own ponds soon followed, but although 3000 persons 'riotously assembled' outside Wyatts' factory in Stroud on 4th June 1825, the strike was generally non-violent.

The strike was briefly successful in halting wage decline but most manufacturers were by then under-capitalised, the money sunk in rebuilding mills between 1800 and 1825 had not been returned in output, and heavy concentration of mills along some Cotswold streams led to difficulties of water supply. Many concerns survived if only just. The half-century from about 1848 was a time of prosperity for those who could respond to increased market demand for Cotswold woollens. But what one manufacturer in this period called 'the palmy days of the Stroud valleys' was achieved at the cost of great poverty in villages like Bisley, unable to mechanise in the same way. Emigration to Brazil, New Zealand, and especially Australia took many people to a new life from the 1830s onwards.

Some mills shifted from wool to metal engineering, developing skills once used to provide machinery for textiles to meet the demand for agricultural machinery. Firms like Lister's of Dursley have their roots in this way. Some, like St Mary's at Chalford, underwent several changes: from cloth- to paper-making between 1846 and 1851, then to a flock mill before turning, for much of this century, to manufacture of umbrella stems and walking sticks.

The growth and popularity of Cheltenham in the eighteenth century brought many people to the Cotswolds. Atkyns considered the place in 1712 'now a greater city than any which the Kingdom contained in the seventeenth century, London alone excepted', but the town's growth, rapid though it was from the later eighteenth century, was much less spectacular than Atkyns would have us believe. People from all over Britain came to take the spa waters. Fosbroke, writing in 1826, saw the High Street as 'but a portion of Bond Street transferred into the country for the convenience of those who like to have the choicest part of London moved elsewhere in the summer months'. Cobbett in 1826 took a very different view of visitors to the spa:

> Cheltenham . . . is what they call a watering place; that is to say, a place to which East India plunderers, West India floggers, English taxgorgers, together with gluttons, drunkards and debauchees of all description, female as well as male, resort, at the suggestion of silently laughing quacks, in the hope of getting rid of the bodily consequences of their manifold sins and iniquities.

Jameson's 1809 *Treatise on Cheltenham Waters and Bilious Diseases* recorded the 'value and medicinal effect' of the waters in each of the wells as an aid to tourists. Yet, even by then, Cheltenham was declining in favour of other spa towns and the town shared in the general decline in Cotswold life in the later nineteenth century.

One commentator on the Cotswold scene in the 1890s noted how 'crumbling mills in half-forgotten valleys, and ruined cottages on her upland pastures, seem to testify to a greatness that has passed away', although she also commented: 'we cannot but hope that the county has a better future in store'. It is precisely because so much of this past survived, of course, that people in later decades were attracted to these crumbling mills in an 'unspoilt' landscape.

CHAPTER 8

The Modern Cotswolds

In the Cotswolds nowadays old mills, barns – even whole farms – are being converted into flats and houses. The Cotswold countryside is represented in magazines and estate agents' advertisements as quintessentially and enduringly English: ordered landscapes, a timeless tranquillity, the epitome of a prized rural 'heritage'. The modern Cotswolds are paradox and problem alike. Having worn its past so well, the area now finds itself being marketed in a way that, if allowed to develop unthinkingly, will threaten the very things that have genuinely survived.

There is a long tradition of topographical writing by tourists and travellers discovering their 'modern' Cotswolds. Drayton's lengthy poem 'Poly-Olbion', written in 1613, has an unlikely description of the life of Cotswold shepherds: 'And, whilst the bag-pipe plays, each lusty jocund swain quaffs sillibubs'. Defoe discerned great virtue in the industriousness of that 'most pleasant and fruitful vale' as he termed the Stroudwater Valley in 1726. Yet not every visitor has warmed to the Cotswolds. Cobbett considered 'The wold . . . an ugly country . . . having less to please the eye than any other that I have seen', and he spoke, too, of its 'yellowish ugly stone'. Sydney Smith, also writing in the early nineteenth century, found the Cotswolds 'one of the most unfortunate, desolate countries under heaven, divided by stone walls, and abandoned to screaming kites and larcenous crows: after travelling really twenty and to appearance ninety miles over this region of stone and sorrow, life begins to be a burden, and you wish to perish'. But the modern view of the Cotswolds has its roots in the 'discovery' of the region by writers and artists (almost without exception strangers to the area) in the early twentieth century.

One book among a number influential in bringing Cotswold life and landscape to the attention of wider audiences was J. Arthur Gibbs' *A Cotswold Village* (1898). Gibbs was born in Somerset in 1868, but by about 1890 had become the squire of

Cheese-rolling on Cooper's Hill (888145) is an old Whit Monday custom more recently transferred to the Spring Bank holiday. It is a very ancient custom indeed and is said to have been a necessary precondition to the maintenance of grazing rights on the common.

the village of Ablington (105078), near Bibury, which is the subject of his book. Gibbs wrote that he sought only 'to record the simple annals of a quiet, old-fashioned Gloucestershire hamlet'. But his work had both a lyrical style and a descriptive accuracy that appealed to those now able, by railway and bike if not yet in any numbers by car, to discover the Cotswolds for themselves. Other books followed: Herbert Evans's *Highways and Byways in Oxford and the Cotswolds* (1905) takes a more romantic view than many (though without being too sentimental); Algernon Gissing's *Broadway* (1904) and his *The Footpath-Way in Gloucestershire* (1924) are nostalgic about the qualities of rural life, real and imagined, even then disappearing.

Artists and craftsmen as well as writers helped create the modern Cotswolds. Some authorities consider that the modern discovery of the Cotswolds can be attributed to the painter and designer William Morris. Morris bought Kelmscot Manor (251989), two miles east of Lechlade, in 1871. Both the house and its surroundings he reckoned 'heaven on earth'. He died there in 1896 and his house is now much as he left it. Morris thought of relocating his London workshops in former silk mills at Blockley (165348) in the north Cotswolds, but was deterred by distance. It was in the Cotswolds, too, that he began the Society for the Protection of Ancient Buildings and Monuments – the 'anti-scrape Society' as it became known. But Morris was not the only one to see in the Cotswolds a quality of life and traditions of craftsmanship and to make them more widely known.

In the early twentieth century, two major groupings of craftsmen keen to maintain and develop local skills in wood and stone settled in the Cotswolds. In the Frome Valley and notably around Sapperton, one group centred around Ernest Gimson, the brothers Ernest and Sidney Barnsley, Norman Jewson, and, to a lesser extent, Detmar Blow and Peter Waals. Further north, the Guild of Handicrafts had been founded in Chipping Campden by C. R. Ashbee in 1902. These men and others like them saw in Cotswolds' workmanship lasting qualities, qualities even then lacking in most urban artisans. Most were architects (Waals was a cabinetmaker and Gimson was best known for his furniture). Together these men not only helped in a small way to sustain the economy of the places they settled in, but, more importantly, helped create through their work on Cotswold houses and churches that lasting sense of tradition and quality in workmanship that permeates the region today.

Gimson lived in and worked from Pinbury Park (955049), once the home of Sir Robert Atkyns and visible in its magnificent setting through the trees on walks east of

Sapperton (it is not open to the public). Toward the end of his life, he lived in and helped restore the medieval Daneway House near Sapperton. Some of his finest work is unfortunately not easily accessible to the public: the stone chimneypiece at Barnsley Park, and the furniture and other work at Rodmarton Manor (942978), made by Ernest Barnsley between 1909 and 1926, although the Cotswold Country Museum and Gallery at Arlington Mill in Bibury has one floor devoted to the Arts and Crafts movement with the work of Gimson, the Barnsleys, and Waals well represented. Both the Barnsleys and Gimson are buried in the churchyard of St. Kenelm's, Sapperton, their graves models of simple dignity beneath the churchyard yews – Gimson to the left and the brothers to the right of the path.

In Chipping Campden, the Arts and Crafts movement centred around C. R. Ashbee. His aims were not only to encourage standards of craftsmanship but, in so doing, to ensure security of employment for the workers. Under Ashbee's influence and leadership, members of the Guild of Handicrafts had moved to Chipping Campden from London. Two years after setting up their workshops in the town, they established the Campden School of Arts and Crafts in which local children and teachers and others from outside were taught woodworking and other skills. The locals perhaps not unnaturally had a rather ambivalent attitude to this intrusion: they derided Ashbee and others for their 'jolly art style of dress', yet prospered as buildings were renovated and income generated. Most credit for the present high quality of the historic buildings in Chipping Campden goes to F. L. Griggs, the engraver and designer. Griggs settled in the town in 1904 following excursions to illustrate Evans's *Highways and Byways*. Evans wrote then 'Let the men of Campden take timely warning, and see to it that their priceless heritage is not lost to them for ever'. Griggs and the Campden Society (later the Campden Trust) were the prime movers in heeding Evans's warning and in ensuring modern innovations like telephone wires did not (and still do not) intrude on Campden's past.

Norman Jewson's *By Chance I Did Rove* has vivid descriptions of Cotswolds village life in the early twentieth century. Jewson had moved to Sapperton in 1907 to work with Gimson and stayed for the next forty years. Amongst his first sights in the Cotswolds was a man ploughing with oxen, for Jewson a classical image: 'I had a feeling that it was a vision from the time of Virgil'. Elsewhere in his autobiography, he recounts the enormous meals – 'farmers ordinaries' – served to farmers on market days in Cirencester, and contrasts this with what he is told by one Billy Bucknell, a native of the tiny hamlet of Tunley (933043) who could remember the 'hungry 'Forties', when the poor had to live on what he called 'barley bangers eked out with mangels stolen from the fields, an occasional trapped rabbit and tea brewed from ground ivy'.

Sapperton, like most other places, had its own sense of identity: 'for the valley even now is a sufficient obstacle to make communication between those living on the opposite sides of it comparatively rare, and to give a very different outlook to those of each side'. Customs were maintained despite the influence of what Jewson called 'glib tongued and flashily dressed' commercial travellers 'who have corrupted the inherited good taste of country folk'. Mummers came round at Christmas and morris dancing was common, though not as widely as in the Oxfordshire Cotswolds. Cecil Sharp travelled widely in the Cotswolds, and many tunes and dances bear local names, especially from the eastern wolds – Idbury Hill, the Longborough Swaggering Boney, the Bledington Hey Away and the Bledington Ladies, also known as Ladies of Pleasure. Jewson and the villagers would have known these songs or variants of them, and it is not impossible that Sharp collected some from the Stroudwater and Golden Valleys: he was certainly in Stroud and Randwick in early April 1908.

Two things in particular brought an end to the Cotswolds of Jewson and Billy Bucknell. The first was the 1914-1918 war, the second the coming of the motor car and the village bus. Aside from the dreadful cost in human life – hardly a village in the Cotswolds is without its memorial cross or a church without its roll of honour – the Great War marked a break in continuity with the past. Traditional skills in building were no longer so widely employed, new materials were used in place of local stone: 'simple ways had gone for ever', wrote Jewson. Strictly speaking, Jewson's claim is untrue. Customs like the dressing of the wells at Bisley, begun by Thomas Keble in 1863 (but much

A study in concentration as the runners in a National Hunt race during the March 1989 Gold Cup week head for the finish at Cheltenham.

older still), cheese-rolling on Cooper's Hill (890145), and the 'clipping' of the church at Painswick continued. Other local ceremonies had disappeared well before 1914. But what is true is that these events have less significance now, less meaning for the places in which they are held, than once they did.

Village bus services were established in the Cotswolds by the late 1920s, although connections were for a long time only between more important villages and market towns. By the later 1930s, charabanc tours from Oxford, Bristol and from Birmingham and the west Midlands especially were a regular feature. One legacy of the Second World War in the Cotswolds is the number of airfields. Some, like Fairford and Brize Norton (290057), are major bases still. Colerne (805714), South Cerney (053988), and Little Rissington (210186) are active bases, but almost nothing remains of the former airfield at Daglingworth, and only slight traces of the runways survive as clues to the position of the airfield north of Chedworth (042128).

In his 1898 *A Cotswold Village* Gibbs, lamenting the state of Cotswold villages after decades of agricultural decline, wrote that 'Without some form of Protection . . . in a hundred years' time these old villages will contain scarcely a single inhabitant', and he continued: 'If only the capitalist or wealthy man of business would take up his abode in these places all might yet be well'. One suspects that Gibbs would be pleased somewhat (if not overly so) at the way his hopes have been realised almost a century later. Large parts of the Cotswolds were recognised as 'Areas of Great Landscape Value' under the provisions of the 1947 Town and Country Planning Act, and in 1966, the Cotswolds were designated an 'Area of Outstanding Natural Beauty'. Yet recognition of the area's scenic and historic qualities has been paralleled by discovery of the region by second-home owners, commuters for whom London, Birmingham and other centres are but an hour or so away by train, and by other men of business Gibbs so hoped would come. In part, this has meant a reworking of the relationships between the established farming society and the newcomers, many of whom work outside but live in the Cotswolds and for whom barns are not 'used' but are converted into homes. The very fact that the modern Cotswolds are so easily accessible has necessitated the keeping of a careful balance between the needs of local people and those attracted to the region from outside, especially where they conflict in 'pressure points' like Bourton-on-the-Water or Broadway on an August Bank Holiday Monday. It is, too, a simple economic fact that reconstituted stone blocks are now more widely used in building than 'real' stone. But, since the 1960s, the work of local councils under the guidance of the Cotswold Building Materials Group has meant that locally-occurring tones in the limestone as well as the widely-employed traditional styles of building are used to ensure Cotswold identity and future continuity with the past.

CHAPTER 9

Cheltenham Spa

Dr Johnson remarked that 'The Man who once ranged the Woods and Climbed the Mountains in Search of Springs of Water for the Good of his Fellow Creatures has undoubtedly merited the Gratitude of Posterity'. If this is the case, Cheltenham has good reason to thank one Henry Skillicorne, who, in 1739, developed as a spa the medicinal spring first utilised in a small way in 1718 by his father-in-law, William Mason, a Cheltenham hosier. Strictly speaking, Cheltenham owes its gratitude to a group of pigeons as much as to Skillicorne: legend has it that the medicinal properties were first noticed after a flock of these birds were seen pecking the mineral salts. Cheltenham also owes its rise as an eighteenth-century spa town – what one observer called 'The merriest sick resort on Earth' – to the publication in 1740 of Dr John Short's *History of Mineral Waters*, and to the five-week visit of George III and the royal family in the summer of 1788. Short's book claimed Cheltenham's waters to be the best in the country; the royal visit conferred a sense of status and prestige upon the town, a sense it is as keen to maintain now as then.

Cheltenham lies at the western edge of the Cotswolds proper but is a good centre from which to discover the Cotswolds as a whole as well as being interesting in its own right. Many of the town's original spa buildings, where they still survive, have been converted to alternative uses, but the town has very fine Regency and early Victorian architecture in many of its town houses, and attractive gardens remain in several places as a legacy of the town's former role.

A good place to start a walk around Cheltenham is the Museum and Art Gallery in Clarence Street, to the north of the bus station. From here, explore southwards via the Promenade towards Imperial Gardens, the Queen's Hotel, and the Montpellier district of town, or northwards by way of the parish church, part of the High Street, and from there to Pittville. Other sites of interest in the town not covered by these two trails are mentioned below.

A choice of routes is available in moving south from the Museum. Turning right from the Museum and then first left leads to St George's Place, one of the oldest streets in the town which follows the line of Stills Lane, a path which once connected the High Street with the Spa Well. Edward Jenner, the pioneer of vaccination, lived in St George's Place from 1795 to 1820; his house, unfortunately, has been demolished. Shaftesbury Hall, situated on the site of a former farm, stands opposite St Matthew's Church, built in 1879, which in turn stands on the site of Cheltenham's manor house, demolished in 1739. Further down St George's Place, a road to the right leads towards St James's Square, once the site of Cheltenham's railway passenger station (closed in 1966), and before that, Jessop's Botanical and Ornithological Gardens. A little further on, the curving line of Royal Well Place will bring you to the rear of the buildings midway along the west side of the Promenade.

Turning left and first right from the Museum will take you into Crescent Place. John Dower House, today the home of the Countryside Commission, was built in 1820 as a boarding house. The Royal Coat of Arms commemorates the residence here of the Duchess of Clarence, wife to William IV. Royal Crescent is a shadow of its former glory. Built between 1806 and 1810, the Crescent once commanded fine views of meadows where buses now stand. The Well Walk, once the most important place to see and be seen in eighteenth-century and Regency Cheltenham, ran from the southern end of what is today Royal Crescent towards the original spa. Cheltenham Ladies College now stands on the line of the Well Walk and the site of Old Well Spa where George III drank medicinal waters: evidently to good effect, too, since we are told by one contemporary diarist that after George III had been to Cheltenham 'he could eat four slices of mutton, and when he came he could only [eat] two'.

From Royal Crescent, cross Royal Well Road and make for the Promenade, either at the southern end of the paved pedestrian precinct or by going to the Imperial Gardens a little uphill and south of the junction with Oriel Road. The Promenade today has a range of expensive shops on its eastern side, Council offices and the Tourist Information Office on the west in buildings still private houses until the early 1900s. The

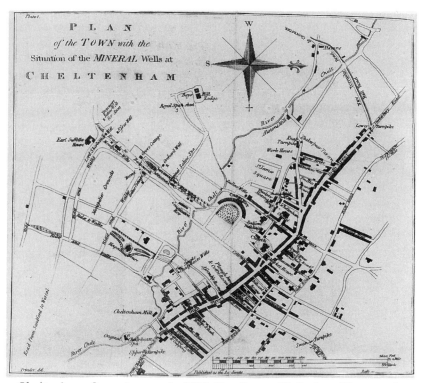

Cheltenham from Jameson's 1809 *Treatise on Cheltenham Waters and Bilious Diseases*, showing the principal mineral wells in the town. Jameson cautioned visitors that '. . . the effect of Cheltenham's waters . . . on the alimentary canal . . . is extremely salutary'.

Promenade was laid out in 1817. It was intended then to be as exclusive as it is in its shops now: access to the Promenade was for subscribers only and neither servants nor dogs were allowed. Originally it was to be called the Colonnade with Roman-style pillars lining the street as the trees do now. The sense of grandeur is real enough without the columns (not erected for reasons of cost): the Promenade was built deliberately wider at the Queen's Hotel end than at the High Street end; the view north is, therefore, of a false perspective: the street was deliberately built to look longer than it is.

The Queen's Hotel stands on the site of the Sherborne Spa, opened in the autumn of 1818 as 'a new Elysium . . . in the

Grecian style' according to Williams's *New Guide to Cheltenham,*
but replaced by the present building in 1837. What are now the
attractively laid-out Imperial Gardens were once Cheltenham's
Winter Gardens, a building of glass and iron built in 1878 and
capable of holding 3,500 persons. The building was knocked
down in 1942; the present gardens quite closely reflect the
original plan.

Montpellier Gardens to the south of the Queen's Hotel now
offer tennis, putting, and even a giant chess board and a
children's gym centre where once they offered 'rides and
walks'. What is now the Lloyds Bank building, known as the
Rotunda and situated at the south end of Montpellier Street,
was erected in 1817 to replace, on the same site, the wooden
Thompson's Spa erected eight years before. The dome was
added in 1825 by the architect John Papworth. The buildings
of Montpellier Walk were constructed in 1836 and have a fine
set of caryatids, armless females in classical style, between the
shopfronts. Both this street and Montpellier Street behind have
a range of good shops, wine bars and restaurants.

Heading back down Montpellier Street will bring you, via a
right turn, to the Queen's Hotel and Imperial Gardens.
Alternatively, from the south end of Montpellier Street, make
your way along Queen's Parade, a fine terrace built in the
1840s, and almost certainly only part of a much larger
development never completed. The building at the west end of
the terrace is new, completed in 1988: a good example of the
sensitive use of local stone in modern building. From here, a
walk down Bayshill Road will bring you to St George's Road
with the buildings of Royal Well Terrace, York Terrace and
Bayshill Terrace on the north side. St George's Place leads back
to Clarence Street and the Museum and Art Gallery.

St Mary's Church, tucked behind the Museum, is the oldest
building in Cheltenham. The oldest stonework dates from the
mid-twelfth century. There is an interesting, and extended,
memorial in the church to Henry Skillicorne; it ends simply:
'He lived and dyed an honest Man'. From the churchyard, go
past the preaching cross and down the short lane into the High
Street, which was for centuries the main and almost the only
major street in Cheltenham: Leland, who in the 1530s
described Cheltenham as 'a longe towne havynge a Market',

Both Pump Room and Pittville Lake are shown as elements in a classical landscape in this engraving from Griffiths' *History of Cheltenham and its Vicinity* (Third edition, 1838).

also knew the town simply as 'Cheltenham Street'. The Lower High Street, to the west of the parish church around Henrietta Street and King Street, was the most important part of pre-Regency Cheltenham. Each of the little streets off it follow the line of burgage or tenement plots, each plot with a building and long garden. In one such narrow street, King Street, the Ebenezer Methodist Chapel built in 1812 still has its original doorway. The Lower High Street was the working-class area of nineteenth-century Cheltenham, and improvements in housing since then have removed or overlain much of interest from that period or earlier.

Any of the streets on the north side of the Lower High Street will lead to Swindon Road. What is now Francis Close Hall here was built as St Paul's Teacher Training College in 1849. Close was an influential evangelical figure in nineteenth-century Cheltenham and was also involved in the establishment in 1841 of Cheltenham College. Rather than making for St Paul's Church by way of St Paul's Street North, take the narrow lane to the east of Francis Close Hall. Like a number in the area, the lane curves as it does because it follows the line of old agricultural holdings, incorporated into street patterns as the land was built upon after the Enclosure Act of 1806. From St Paul's Church, built c.1829, go east along St Paul's Road towards Clarence Square and Pittville. Pittville gates at the east end of Clarence Road mark the entrance to Pittville, now part of Cheltenham but originally intended in the 1820s as 'the nucleus of a second town, rivalling its parent Cheltenham both in extent and importance'. Near Pittville Gates, at 4 Clarence Road, is the Holst Birthplace Museum. The house is much more than a museum to Gustav Holst, the composer who wrote *The Planets*, and has several rooms interestingly furnished in the styles of the Regency and Victorian periods.

Pittville takes its name from Joseph Pitt, a lawyer and MP for Cricklade who, from 1824, created the estate and gardens that bear his name, using as his architect John Forbes, and for the walks and rides one Richard Ware. Walking north from Pittville Gates towards the lake and Pittville Pump Room is to see some very splendid villa houses. Regency Lodge, built c.1835, and the last building on the east side of Pittville Lawn before crossing Central Cross Drive, is a fine example. The Long Garden and Pittville Lawn lead to the Lake and the Pump Room beyond.

Begun in 1825, at a ceremony noted for 'the ringing of bells, the firing of cannon and other rejoicing', the Pump Room became Cheltenham's grandest spa and is the venue for concerts and exhibitions today. The upper floors house displays of costume and other artefacts from Cheltenham's Regency past. Across the Evesham Road, the modern pleasure seeker can choose from boating on the lake, tennis or the pitch and putt course, and a little way north on this road will bring you to Cheltenham Racecourse, where the Gold Cup meeting in particular brings thousands each year. Cheltenham Races, begun in 1819 by the Duke of Gloucester, have not always been held here. They were formerly run on the downlands of Cleeve Hill, beyond the scarp edge of Cleeve Cloud which overlooks the village of Prestbury and the modern racecourse. Festivals of music, literature, and cricket also provide today much of what past visitors to Cheltenham would have sought in entertainment. Those who want to taste the spa waters can do so at the Pittville Pump Room or at the Town Hall near

Giles Grinagain's 1802 cartoon, 'The Rapid Effects of Cheltenham Waters', caricatured the consequences of too much medicinal water!

Imperial Gardens. Those who would rather swim in Cheltenham water than drink it have the indoor Pittville Pool or, in summer, the outdoor pool at Sandford Park off Keynsham Road, south off the A40 London/Oxford road.

There are many walks and splendid views of the town and beyond on the hills of the scarp edge surrounding Cheltenham. Cleeve Hill and Cleeve Cloud (984265), to the north of Cheltenham on the B4632 (was the A46), offer wonderful views in all directions, especially north-westwards across the vale to the Malvern Hills. There are several archaeological sites of interest here: 'The Ring' (985266) is a small Iron Age enclosure; the 'Cross Dyke', a little to the south, is an Iron Age bank and ditch nearly 600 metres in length; and further south still are the remains of Cleeve Hill Camp (985255), whose walls have in places been disturbed by quarrying and the golf course.

Nottingham Hill (984283), reached by turning left at the brow of the hill past Cleeve Hill (opposite the golf course entrance), is also an Iron Age hillfort. From here, walks lead off and down towards the villages of Prescott (where car enthusiasts hold hill climbs), Gotherington, and Woodmancote. To the south of Cheltenham, Leckhampton Hill (950183) and the nearby Charlton King's Common are popular places for walks. The Iron Age hillfort at Leckhampton has lost its north and west ramparts as a result of quarrying; the stone has been worked here since at least the reign of Edward III (1327-1369), and many of Cheltenham's finest 'ceremonial' buildings from the town's heyday as a spa are built of Leckhampton stone. In Leckhampton village, now part of Cheltenham, several seventeenth-century cottages still survive.

Crickley Hill (933163), further south from Leckhampton Hill on the B4070, is a country park with ecological, geological, and archaeological trails, and in the latter context, the site is of considerable importance in British prehistory. The positions of the several settlements to have occupied the hill are shown by the use of coloured posts sunk in the ground and by displays of diagrams. The earliest settlement here dates from before 4,000BC. Although the site was deserted after the Neolithic period for perhaps a thousand years, we know there was a hillfort here about 650BC. A second followed in about 500BC and the Romans had a small farm near here to the east. Under the guidance of the Crickley Trust, Gloucestershire County Council and other bodies, excavations continue every year on this important site, and work permitting, it is possible to be shown the dig.

Belas Knap Long Barrow (021254) is another prehistoric site of interest in the area and may be reached from the track leading off the minor road between Charlton Abbots and Winchcombe or, in a longer walk, by following the footpath indicated where the minor road past Whitehall Farm ends at West Down (010236). The Roman villa in Spoonley Wood (045257) is worth a visit for those who like to come across their antiquities the hard way: not an easy walk for young children and not to be done without wellingtons. Much easier to get to are the Roman villa sites near Great Witcombe (899142) and at Chedworth (052136).

Witcombe villa was discovered in 1818. The building itself dates from the mid-third century AD and seems to have been

The late twelfth-century church of St John's at Elkstone, seen from the south east.

occupied until the fifth century. There is a small museum here of finds from the villa.

Chedworth villa is one of the best preserved Roman villas in Britain. Although it is well situated in a sheltered site of good aspect and with a spring, the Romans also terraced the west and north ranges of this extensive building. The remains of baths of various temperatures, the tiled floors, and the surviving hypocausts of the Roman domestic heating system are particularly interesting. There is a museum of finds from the villa and an audio-visual display in the visitor centre run by the National Trust. More remains to be known of Chedworth villa: the south range extends much further east than the currently-exposed sections, but financial restrictions hinder excavation. Near the entrance to the villa, a flight of steps leads to the Chedworth Nature Reserve, owned and managed by the Gloucestershire Trust for Nature Conservation, and of interest for its wildlife and geology.

The houses making up Chedworth village are scattered along

the valley sides south of Chedworth woods. The church, St Andrew's, is late Norman and has a very fine fifteenth-century stone pulpit. The church at Stowell (089130), a little to the north-east, has important wall paintings of the late twelfth century. The extensive mansion and park here date from c.1600. The house is impressively situated with good views to the west across to Yanworth and along the Coln Valley.

Withington (031155) is situated on a bend in the Coln river and is an attractive village whose church tower may be seen from some miles away, especially by travellers following the line of the road running north-west of the village. Minor roads out of Withington lead towards Compton Abdale to the east or, to the west, the villages of Colesbourne (001132) and Cowley (984147).

Compton Abdale (065168) stands on the White Way, a trackway dating from the Neolithic period, which follows the high ground in its north-south route through the Cotswolds. From the village, cross the A40 and follow the line of another historic line of communication, the Salt Way, before turning right towards the hamlet of Salperton (078202). This settlement derived its past importance (and name) from its involvement with the passing salt trade. Most of its buildings today are seventeenth or eighteenth century in date.

North of the A436, and, like Salperton, east of the Salt Way, is the village of Hawling (065231), which at one time extended further eastwards than it does today. The remains of former house plots, the result of clearance for sheep in the medieval period, may be seen in fields to the north of the lane leading to Guiting Power and on both sides of Campden Lane north of the village.

West of Hawling, a minor road on the west of the valley connects the villages of Charlton Abbots (032242), Brockhampton (034224), and Sevenhampton (033218). Both the first and the last of these have fine sixteenth-century manor houses: Brockhampton Park, dating from about 1640, has been converted into luxury flats. Continuing south down this road brings you to Syreford and the small but attractive village of Whittington (014209). The church here, St Bartholomew's, has a lovely, plain, early thirteenth-century font and brasses from the mid-1550s, but the chief attraction of the village, apart from some of the sixteenth-century cottages, is Whittington Court, a splendid example of an unfortified Cotswold manor house. There has been considerable continuity of settlement here: the house stands on the site of a Roman villa and a moated settlement. The moat survives in part. From Whittington, a narrow lane leads west past Ham Hill and runs through the tiny settlement of Ham towards Cheltenham. South of the A40 from Whittington are the villages of Dowdeswell, Andoversford, and Kilkenny. Dowdeswell (001198) is prettily situated on a south-west facing hillside. The church of St. Michael's is well worth a visit and has a fine Norman tympanum. Kilkenny, reached by a lane to the south of Dowdeswell, is a small hamlet where the A436 divides to head for Stow or, after joining the A40, Oxford. Past the Frog Mill Inn, in the field to the left as the A436 meets the A40 (028184), the remains of the once more extensive village of Shipton Solers are now visible as bumps and hollows. The main street, running more or less parallel with the modern A40 and now a long hollow, can be easily made out.

Just west of Kilkenny, a minor road left leads through Hilcot towards Colesbourne in the Churn Valley. The park here has a good collection of rare trees, the result of careful selection and management in the 1860s. Cowley, off the A435, has a fine Italianate manor, largely a mid-Victorian creation, with attractive terraces and a lake best seen from the south. The church at Cowley dates from the early thirteenth century.

One of the finest of all Cotswold churches is St John's at Elkstone (868122). It is important because it retains its original, aisleless, twelfth-century form in all essentials with the exception of the fifteenth-century west tower. It is a lovely church, in a village now notable for having had its main farm buildings converted into houses. The carving is of wonderful quality throughout, the grotesques especially, and the columbarium, dovecote, over the chancel is a very rare feature indeed. From Elkstone, the road leads south towards Cirencester or north back to Cheltenham and, from there, to Winchcombe.

CHAPTER 10

Winchcombe and the North-West Wold-Edge Villages

Winchcombe (025282), about seven miles north-east of Cheltenham on the B4632 (formerly the A46), is an ancient Saxon borough. The town ruled the Saxon kingdom of Hwicce, part of Mercia, and in 787, Offa the King of Mercia established a nunnery in the town. A later Saxon King, Coenulf or Kenulf, founded an Abbey here in 798 and until c.1017 when the area was incorporated into Gloucestershire, Winchcombe was capital of its own shire, Wincelcumbeshire. The town's prosperity in wool and as a centre of pilgrimage suffered with the destruction of the abbey in 1539. Although Winchcombe's fortunes revived in the seventeenth century when it was the centre for tobacco growing in Gloucestershire – a trade commemorated in the names Tobacco Close and Tobacco Field – the town's more recent role as a local market centre has left many fine buildings, sacred and secular, relatively untouched.

Nothing now remains of the Abbey. St Peter's Church, built about 1465, was in part restored more than once during the nineteenth century. It is a lovely building, one of the finest Perpendicular churches in the Cotswolds. In the west end are two stone coffins, thought to be those of King Kenulf and his son, St Kenelm. On the north wall hangs an embroidered altar cloth attributed to Katherine of Aragon, and, in the corner, a rather crudely-fashioned cello formerly used in Gretton Old Church (006305). In the summer months, stewards are usually present in St Peter's to answer questions.

In the main square south of the church, the Jacobean house, built in 1618, is a good example of a merchant's house of that time. Immediately to the south of this house are the Chandos Almshouses built in 1573 but partly restored since. From these buildings follow the main road, Gloucester Street, towards the Corner Cupboard Inn, a sixteenth-century building (reputedly haunted) on the corner of Malthouse Lane. Number 23 Gloucester Street is the home of the Winchcombe Railway Museum. From Malthouse Lane, turn right along Back Lane.

90

Butcher's shop-front at the Cross, Winchcombe, next door to the George Hotel, c.1870. Note the carcasses hung out.

Remnants of the earthwork walls of Saxon Winchcombe can be traced along Back Lane. North Street has a range of building styles and dates; the White Lion, one of the most interesting, dates from the seventeenth century. The Town Hall at the junction of North Street and High Street has a small Folk Museum and a Police Museum and is the Tourist Information Centre. Left from the Town Hall takes you into Hailes Street, and almost opposite is the sixteenth-century George Hotel with the initials of Richard Kidderminster, the penultimate Abbot of Winchcombe, carved in the heads of the doorposts. Most buildings in Hailes Street date from the sixteenth century although the original timber framing in some is now supported, if not replaced, by stone. The houses in Abbey Terrace are later in date, although the nineteenth-century front of Bleby House hides interior evidence of earlier work. From Abbey Terrace, pass down attractive tree-lined Vineyard Street and follow the signs to Sudeley Castle (032278).

The earliest buildings at Sudeley date from the fifteenth century when the Castle was owned by one Ralph Boteler, but the present house is very largely the creation in the mid-sixteenth century of Admiral Lord Seymour and his wife Katherine Parr, widow of Henry VIII. She died at Sudeley and her tomb is in the Castle chapel. After the Civil War, the Castle was 'slighted', i.e. rendered uninhabitable with the roofs removed, and much of the original building was demolished in 1649. Used as a quarry for building stone by local inhabitants, Sudeley was bought in 1837 by the brothers John and William Dent, and it is to them and their descendants that Sudeley owes its present condition. The house contains a fine collection of paintings including works by J. M. W. Turner and John Constable, and the letters of Emma Dent give a fascinating insight into well-to-do Victorian country life. The gardens are nineteenth-century and the work of the Dents, although the design of the Queen's Garden closely follows the formal geometric patterns of the original Tudor parterre. For twentieth-century children there is an adventure playground, and whilst several musical and theatrical events are held in the house or gardens during the year, few things equal the falconry displays for grace and skill. For those who want to stay longer, the old estate cottages have been converted into luxury holiday accommodation.

On leaving Sudeley Castle grounds, turn right rather than heading back to Winchcombe. Stay on this minor road which is quite steep as it climbs the scarp; it follows the Salt Way along the top of the hill. The wall on the western edge, though modern in form, follows the line of the Outer Park Wall (054265), the upper boundary of a former medieval sheep park. Turn left at the Roel Gate crossroads and make for the village of Guiting Power (093248). As you pass by Roel farm, look out for the turf mounds in adjacent fields; these are the remains of Roel village, cleared of its people in the medieval period to make way for the more profitable sheep.

Guiting Power centres around a large village green and is a rather quiet and withdrawn place despite its location on a through road. For the more energetic, the footpath to the village of Naunton makes a pleasant walk; motorists may take the minor road south and follow the A436 for a very short way before turning off towards Naunton, or follow the lanes past Guiting Stud and Grange Hill Farm. Naunton (115236) is strung out along both sides of the River Windrush with most houses on the northern side of the valley. St Andrew's Church stands at the west end of the village, and besides two fine

This early fourteenth-century wall painting of St Catherine of Alexandria in one of the window splays on the eastern wall of the nave in Hailes church depicts her as a courtly and learned figure.

sundials and an interesting eighteenth-century notice about funds disbursed for estate maintenance, the church's most interesting feature is its richly decorated pulpit dating from c.1400. From the church, cross the bridge and turn right to the main part of the village. Cromwell House is early seventeenth century in date and, in part, of rubble construction. Almost the last house in the village is Naunton Mill, which was converted into a private dwelling in the mid-1960s. A little to the west of the Black Horse Inn, a gravel path leads to a bridge across the river and a narrow lane, often muddy even in summer, runs along the southern bank of the Windrush and across meadows back to the church.

From Naunton, make for Temple Guiting (095282) either by going through the small villages of Barton and Kineton or, in following the A436 for a short way, by taking the first minor road left. The Cotswold Farm Park is just off this road (112269). This Farm Park has the most comprehensive collection of rare breeds of British farm animals in the country. Apart from its scientific importance in connection with the Rare Breeds Survival Trust, the Park and its animals will delight children and adults alike. Temple Guiting, as the name suggests, was once held by the Order of the Knights Templar. The original Norman church has been rather spoilt by several later improvements, but in Manor Farm further down the lane from the church, the village boasts a fine Cotswold Tudor farmhouse.

From Temple Guiting, go northwards and at Ford (085294) turn left along the B4077 towards Stumps Cross (076303). There are views here of Bredon Hill and the Vale of Evesham, and several footpaths lead off from this point, either down the scarp towards Beckbury hillfort and the abbey and church at Hailes, toward Wood Stanway and beyond, or east towards Taddington and Cutsdean.

What little remains of Hailes Abbey (050300) is impressive enough. The Abbey, a Cistercian house, was founded in 1246 by Richard, Earl of Cornwall and younger brother of Henry III. In 1270, Richard's son Edmund brought to Hailes a relic of the Holy Blood with the guarantee from the Patriarch of Jerusalem, later Pope Urban IV, that it was genuinely the blood of Christ. The possession of such a relic made Hailes a great centre of pilgrimage. At the Dissolution, the relic was declared to be 'honey clarified and coloured with saffron' and was destroyed. Standing on the raised mound of grass that was the site of the high altar gives a good idea of the extent of the former Abbey church. The shrine and the five chapels at the east end were all built as later additions to the church to house the Blood of Hailes.

Part of the extensive remains of the Cistercian Hailes Abbey, looking roughly west through the cloisters. More of the monastic buildings would have survived had they not been plundered as building material after the abbey's dissolution in 1539.

All of the other buildings are labelled and there is a very good museum with colourful displays of the architecture and past life at Hailes. What is now a ruin was once a centre of learning and worship, and, as elsewhere, the surrender of the Abbey on Christmas Eve 1539 brought the life of a whole community to a close.

Perhaps because of its size and position, the church at Hailes has a simple and appealing dignity. It should not be missed. The church, which has no dedication, was built sometime in the early twelfth century. The rood screen is fifteenth-century, as is the stained glass, but the church's real glory is its wall paintings of c.1300. On entering, the large figure on the wall opposite is St Christopher, staff in hand, bearing the child Christ on his shoulder. On the south wall is a wonderful hunting scene with leaping hounds and a hare cowering beneath a bush. Other paintings in this delightful church are of saints, heraldic devices and fabulous creatures from the medieval bestiaries.

From Hailes, make for Stanway (061321) either by following the B4632 and the B4077 or by going through Didbrook and

Wood Stanway. If coming by the latter route, look for the ridge and furrow of former field systems in the fields to the right of the road. Just to the east of Toddington crossroads (050324), the Gloucestershire Warwickshire Steam Railway runs regular steam trains between Toddington and Winchcombe. In due course, this line will be re-opened to connect Cheltenham Racecourse and Broadway.

Stanway has a lot to interest in a small area. The most obvious feature is the impressive Gatehouse, built c.1630 by Timothy Strong of Barrington and not, as was long thought, by Inigo Jones. The tithe barn has a simpler grandeur. Built about 1370 by the Abbots of Tewkesbury to store their tithes, the barn was restored in 1927 and is used today for dances and theatrical performances. Stanway House was built by the Tracy family in the sixteenth century on the site of an earlier building. Inside, a large landscape painting of 1748 by William Taylor of Worcester shows Stanway as it would have looked at that time. The ornamental water in the foreground was drained in the early nineteenth century. There is some fine Chelsea porcelain in the house and one of only three surviving complete shuffleboard tables (a type of shove-ha'penny). The church, St Peter's, dates from the twelfth century.

From Stanway, the clearly-marked footpath to Stanton makes a pleasant walk. The ridges and furrows on the small cricket pitch here must make for exciting games!

Stanton village (069342) was much restored in 1927, but sympathetically so, and is charming if much frequented. Some of the houses here have dated inscriptions above the doorway; look for the 'T W 1577' on the doorway of the Manorway. Stanton Court dates from the early seventeenth century. At the far end of the village, a footpath leads out of the corner of the car park from the Mount Inn up a sunken way towards Snowshill, and there are wonderful views from the top as reward.

Following this path and the narrow roads from the top will bring the walker to Snowshill, but the motorist must take the main road towards Broadway (095375). Clear away the cars and the shop signs, imagine its main streets freer of people, and the beauty of Broadway's buildings, especially in the High Street, would show almost better than anywhere else the skill of

Cotswold masons working in traditional styles. This same style and character have long attracted visitors to Broadway, although, of course, the residents can't live off rustic charm alone. On summer days, one can't but wonder if the Cotswolds town was named after its resemblance to the thoroughfare in New York. The Lygon Arms Hotel in the centre of the village dates from about 1620 although there are parts of earlier date. The Abbot's Grange to the west of the small green on the corner with Church Street is fourteenth century and was part of the holdings of Pershore Abbey. Rather than going up the High Street and continuing up Fish Hill to get to Broadway Tower Country Park, continue up Church Street in the direction of Snowshill. About a mile from Broadway on this road is St Eadburgha's Church, dedicated to King Alfred's grand-daughter. The church is basically Norman and, although over-restored in 1866, there is a fine fourteenth-century carved wooden pulpit and a font, perhaps pre-Norman in age, without decoration. From the church, continue up the hill to Snowshill.

Snowshill (097337), and more particularly Snowshill Manor, is a popular place with visitors but without the crowds of Broadway. The cottages grouped around St Barnabas's Church and up the minor roads to the south have a richer-coloured stone than in some villages. The church has a fine Jacobean pulpit c.1640 but is otherwise rather dull.

In some ways a typical early sixteenth-century manor house, Snowshill Manor also exhibits classical details of c.1720 in its south front, and, in some of its interior fittings, has features more characteristic of the neo-Tudor style of the early twentieth century than the sixteenth. The house was bought in 1919 by Charles Wade who spent most of the rest of his life collecting its fascinating contents. The house and its contents were gifted to the National Trust in 1951. The contents are extraordinary in their variety: Chinese vases, Italian furniture, nautical memorabilia, Samurai armour, a collection of children's prams from 1750 to 1900; something for everyone, in fact. After viewing all that's here, it is almost vital to rest in the terraced gardens before continuing.

From Snowshill, take the minor road that leads out of the village from behind the church and head for Broadway Tower Country Park (113360). There are signposted nature trails and walks, play areas and glorious views over twelve counties from the Park. The tower is an eighteenth-century folly built of limestone from further east, hence the darker colour. William Morris and other Pre-Raphaelites used to holiday here, and it was from the Tower in 1876 that Morris wrote the letter that was to lead to the foundation of the Society for the Protection of Ancient Buildings and Monuments. From the Country Park, cross the A44 and go down the scarp edge towards Saintbury (118398). The church here, St Nicholas's, is off the main road up a metalled path but is worth stopping to visit for its Saxon sundial on the south wall and the graceful spire. Continuing down the hill brings you to the A46. From the junction, turn right for Weston-Subedge and Stratford-upon-Avon or left to Willersey, at one time the summer holiday retreat of the Abbots of Evesham. From Willersey, the road leads south to Broadway.

CHAPTER 11

Chipping Campden and the North Cotswolds

On the south side of the canopy of the tomb to Sir Baptist and Lady Hicks in Chipping Campden's St James's Church is an inscription whose first line reads (in translation), 'O fortunate Campden, you possess great treasure'. And so it does.

Campden's beauty in its houses, churches, and in its high street – what one historian has called 'The most beautiful village street now left in the island' – is, in part, the result of the town's involvement in the medieval wool trade. In part also, Campden has benefited as many Cotswold towns have not from the attention of modern conservationists. Important in this respect was the Guild of Handicrafts, set up in Chipping Campden in 1902 (although it had been located in London's Mile End since its foundation in 1888), and the Campden Society, founded in 1924. This latter body formed the Campden Trust in 1929 and it is to these institutions and to F. L. Griggs in particular that Campden owes its lack of overhead telephone wires and electric cables and the preservation '. . . of the beauty and character of the town'.

St James's Church, up Church Street at the east end of the High Street, is amongst the finest of the Cotswold 'wool' churches. But whereas places like Northleach have John Fortey, and Fairford John Tame, as benefactors, the situation for Chipping Campden is a little less clear. One wool merchant who would like to be remembered is William Grevel whose memorial brass, in the floor of the chancel, states that he was 'The flower of the wool merchants of all England'. His house still stands in the High Street and is notable for its two-storey Perpendicular window. But although Grevel left money for 'new work' to be done to St James', it is likely that more was done with monies received from other less well-known Campden wool merchants like William Weoley and John Bradway. Bradway died in 1488, leaving funds for the 'Bylding of the nave and body of the church'. The result of these miscellaneous benefactions is a church of great harmony and unity in style.

99

The nave is magnificent and is so similar to that of Northleach that it is likely the two are the work of one man. Apart from the Grevel brass, other items of interest include the late fifteenth-century Flemish brass lectern, gifted to the church by Sir Baptist Hicks in 1618, the Jacobean pulpit (also a gift from Hicks, in 1612), displays of documents relating to the town and church in the past (beneath the tower and in the muniments room above the south porch), and, in the south or Gainsborough Chapel, the memorial effigies of Sir Baptist Hicks himself and his wife, Lady Elizabeth.

Hicks, who became Viscount Campden one year before his death in 1629, made gifts to the town as well as the church. The fine almshouses on the north-west side of Church Street were built with funds from Hicks in 1612. These buildings, sensitively restored in 1953, have been considered by one architectural historian 'the crowning achievement of the domestic Cotswold style and mason-craft of the early seventeenth century'. Opposite, and partly obscured by high walls, are the remains of Hicks's home, Campden House, destroyed by Royalist troops in the Civil War. Two pavilions, the lodges and the gateway still stand, the last just south of the entrance to the church.

From Church Street, the High Street opens out to the west. A right turn here towards Cider Mill Lane and Leysbourne (the houses on the north side of the road) leads to the small Wilson Memorial Garden, opened in 1984 to commemorate the botanical work abroad of Ernest 'Chinese' Wilson, born in Campden in 1876. From here, it is possible to walk round the back of the town along Back Ends and see how Campden's houses have followed the plots of the medieval burgage strips, or to turn back along the High Street.

William Grevel's house, built about 1380, is on the north side of the High Street, almost opposite Church Street. A little further along on the south side is the Woolstaplers' Hall, built for Robert Calf, one of the town's wool merchants in the late fourteenth century. The building was renovated by C. R. Ashbee for the Guild of Handicrafts but has more recently been a museum with displays of local and wider interest. Bedfont House is a superb eighteenth-century town house, built in the 1740s by Thomas Woodward for the Cotterell

The crowded scene at Chipping Campden sheep market, c.1900.

family. Continuing on the south side, you will pass the nineteenth-century Lygon Arms, the attractive eighteenth-century Dover's House, and the buildings of the Old Grammar School. On the north side, the gentle curve of the terrace is attractive as a whole: interesting individual buildings include The Martins, dating from about 1714, and, further on past the Market Hall, the Regency styling of the Cotswold House Hotel.

The Market Hall in Market Place was built by Hicks in 1627 for the marketing of cheese, butter and poultry. The sheep fairs were held in the Market Place itself. Further west, the High Street narrows as it nears its junction with Sheep Street. At the west end of the High Street, Hoo Lane leads towards Dover's Hill (139389).

Dover's Hill takes its name from Robert Dover, a Norfolk-born lawyer who, having moved to the area (he lived at nearby Saintbury), began the festivities here that became known as Dover's Games. It may be that some sort of annual games were in existence before Dover's involvement began in 1612, but the Games here bore his name until they ended in 1852. These Cotswold 'Olimpicks' changed over the years: horse racing and hare coursing with greyhounds were popular at first; music, dancing and feasting were popular at all times; and the 'sport' of shin-kicking was much contested in the nineteenth century.

The Games have been twice defunct: from Dover's death in 1652 until the Restoration of Charles II in 1660, and again from 1852 (when stopped by zealous clergymen campaigning against the by then 'low moral tone' of the games) until their revival in the Festival of Britain in 1951.

North of Chipping Campden, the names of villages like Aston Subedge (139415) give notice of the change from hill to vale. Burnt Norton, near Aston, inspired the poem of that name by T. S. Eliot. Mickleton (162435) has a lovely building in Medford House (just before the turn-off to the church on the right) and several walks up the scarp towards Kiftsgate Court, but is otherwise unremarkable. But just on the edge of the hills the hamlets of Hidcote Bartrim and Hidcote Boyce are more attractive. Hidcote House standing between the two is a good late seventeenth-century survival, and at Hidcote Manor (175429) there are lovely formal gardens open to the public. Further east still, the village of Ilmington (210434) sits on the very northern edge of the Cotswolds.

South-east of Chipping Campden is the small village of Broad Campden (160378), which, like its more famous namesake, is seen to advantage from the hills on the Blockley Road as it runs west of Northwick Park. The mansion at Northwick Park, which is itself best seen from the minor road to the north-west of the estate, was built in 1686 and is now a centre for local business enterprises. Either of these two roads from Broad Campden leads to the small town of Blockley (165350), sunk in a hollow in the hills, the Dovedale Valley. In the late eighteenth century, Blockley was a centre for the manufacture of silk, but the industry had ceased by the late 1880s. The town has several attractive terraces of houses, and, in places, the pavements have been raised above the narrow streets. South of Blockley (take the B4479 and the A44) is the village of Bourton-on-the-Hill (175325), which has to be one of the Cotswold villages most in need of a bypass. The traffic roars through the village, but the church, St Lawrence's, is worth stopping to visit (there is a very interesting standard bushel and peck measure kept in the church, of the type abandoned in 1826 on introduction of Imperial measures), and a tithe barn dated 1570 further down the hill.

Near to Bourton are two of the finest gardens in the

The graceful lines of the west tower of St James's church in Chipping Campden overshadow the Jacobean lodges and gateway to the now-vanished Campden House.

Cotswolds. Batsford Arboretum (183337), which may be entered via a minor road off the A44 east of Bourton, was laid out by Ernest George in 1888 for the then Lord Redesdale. The lie of the land here, with limestone soils on the Great Oolite shading downhill into the clay lands to the east, has allowed a range of species to thrive. A little larger than Westonbirt to the south, the garden at Batsford benefits from its hilly aspect and has many delights in its trees and shrubs. In May, the 'pocket-handkerchief' tree, (*Davidia involucrata*) is amongst the highlights here. The mansion at Batsford, though built in the Elizabethan style, is contemporary with the garden. After selling Batsford, the Redesdales moved to Swinbrook in the Windrush Valley.

If Batsford owes much in its design to Japanese influences (Lord Redesdale was a diplomat in Tokyo), then the gardens and house at Sezincote (172311) are north India come to the Cotswolds. The main entrance to Sezincote is directly opposite the driveway to Batsford. The house at Sezincote is the result, in combination, of the work of Sir Charles Cockerell, his brother Samuel Pepys Cockerell, and the topographical artist

Thomas Daniell, the last of whom was the most knowledgeable European in his day about Indian architecture. The house, built c.1805, is a mixture of Hindu and Moslem detail. The golden glow of the stone used may, however, be the result of staining: the stone from the quarry used, at Bourton-on-the-Hill, is not naturally that colour.

The garden has a number of Indian features, notably the Indian Bridge with its balustrade of Brahmin bulls and the temple to Suraya, the Hindu sun god. Sezincote is thought to be the only Moghul building that has survived in western Europe: with its domed roof and Indian imagery, it is certainly unique in the Cotswolds.

Moreton-in-Marsh (205325) was founded in 1226 by the Abbot of Westminster at a crossroads on the Fosse Way with a major road between London and Worcester. The imposing Town or Redesdale Hall in the centre of the High Street, though built in the medieval fashion, dates only from 1887 and is the work of Ernest George. The houses flanking both sides of the High Street mostly date from the late eighteenth and nineteenth centuries. Probably the oldest building in Moreton is the Curfew Tower on the corner of the High Street with Oxford Street. The building is sixteenth century and the bell dates to about 1635; look on the High Street side for a list of tolls charged in the town in 1905. Further out of town on the A44 towards Oxford is the Fire Training College and, at a slight bend in the road, the Four Shires Stone marks the meeting point of counties (only three since Worcestershire's boundaries were redrawn in 1931).

North of Moreton, the Fosse Way (A429) runs out of the Cotswolds towards the flatter and wetter lands of the Midlands. Villages like Stretton-on-Fosse (222382) and the more distant and larger town of Shipston-on-Stour (258405) show in their mixture of red brick and Cotswold stone buildings that these places lie on the very northern fringes of the Cotswolds.

CHAPTER 12

Stow-on-the-Wold and the Oxfordshire Wolds

East from Stow-on-the-Wold and across the valley of the Evenlode towards Chipping Norton and Wychwood Forest, the country is more open than in some other parts of the Cotswolds. Further east than Chipping Norton – self-styled 'Gateway to the Cotswolds' – many of the villages begin to lose that unity of style and stone that marks the district proper.

Stow-on-the-Wold (192255) stands on one of the highest points of the eastern plateau. Even on summer days, its position exposes it to often chilling breezes: in 1762, five soldiers are said to have died of exposure after being caught in a blizzard near the town, and there is a local saying that 'at Stow-on-the-Wold the devil caught cold'. Stow (originally 'Edwardsstowe') was granted a market in 1107, but the importance of the site is evident in the earlier founding of a monastery there and in the remains of Roman and Iron Age settlements. Today, Stow is a well-to-do, even rather prim, little town. Most buildings and things of interest in the town are in the vicinity of The Square, east of the A429 (the Fosse Way), and north of Sheep Street, the A436 to Chipping Norton.

The market cross in the south-east corner of The Square was renovated in 1878 to record the thanks of the town to Joseph Chamberlayne whose gift of £1000 allowed Stow to have regular supplies of clean water for the first time. In the centre of The Square, the Gothic Revival St Edward's Hall sits rather uncomfortably with the surrounding buildings. The King's Arms is one of the most interesting buildings on the east side. It is a good example of the many inns and coaching houses that made Stow a wealthy market town in the past. In 1548, Edward VI reckoned this the best inn between London and Worcester, and Royal patronage continued when Charles I stayed in 1645. The east side of The Square ends in the village green with its village stocks (the present ones are nineteenth-century in date). From the green, cross over, and, to the rear of a row of shops, take the lane that leads to St Edward's Church.

Like St John's at Burford, this church was used to house prisoners during the Civil War. The north porch, a seventeenth-century addition to a building chiefly fourteenth- and fifteenth-century in date, is framed by two yews that seem almost to support the church itself. From the church, the lane enters Church Street near the late sixteenth-century Masonic Hall, formerly St Edward's Grammar School. Church Street leads either back to The Square or to eastwards-sloping Sheep Street. Most of the buildings in Sheep Street are seventeenth or eighteenth century (though many have later and not always attractive frontages). From the car park at the east end, a footpath and a minor road lead to Maugersbury, now a tiny hamlet but older as a settlement than Stow.

To the south-west of Stow, the Slaughters (Upper and Lower) are connected by the River Eye. Upper Slaughter (155232) has the remains of a substantial castle evident as a mound just east of the village church and a number of attractive houses grouped around an open square. Yet it lacks something of the formal picturesque qualities of its namesake, Lower Slaughter (165225). The finest single building here is the Manor House, built by Valentine Strong (one of the many Strongs of Barrington and Taynton fame) in about 1650. The village itself, west of the manor house and lying along both banks of the shallow-flowing Eye, is very pleasing. The village ends at the pond and water wheel of a nineteenth-century corn mill which, surprisingly for a brick building, does not seem too incongruous here.

Closer to Stow are the smaller villages of Lower and Upper Swell. The river here, the Dikler, rises to the north near Bourton-on-the-Hill but flows underground before surfacing in the lake now used by Donnington Brewery (173278). Most of the buildings at Lower Swell (172255) and Upper Swell (176269) are eighteenth-century, but Abbotswood (off the B4077 from Stow and in its present form dating from 1902) is considered to be Sir Edwin Lutyens' principal work in the Cotswolds. Nether Swell Manor, built c.1910, is amongst the best work of Dawber who also built nearby Eyford Park (west of the A436), and, farther north, the house and arboretum at Batsford.

From Stow, the A436 crosses the Evenlode Valley to connect

Fair Day at Stow-on-the-Wold in 1900.

with the A44 before entering Chipping Norton. From Chipping Norton, it is possible to visit the north-eastern corner of the Cotswolds around Great Rollright, the Rollright stones and Hook Norton and even to go on towards places like Bloxham before turning south again on the A361 to visit the Wychwoods and the Oxfordshire Wolds. Alternatively, follow the minor roads along the valley of the Evenlode towards Milton-under-Wychwood, and Shipton-under-Wychwood, and from there take the A361 to Chipping Norton and the places beyond.

Immediately east of Stow is a scattering of small villages well worth a visit. Broadwell (208274) is centred around a large triangular village green with a small ford to the south-east. Up the hill toward the church of St Paul's (which, like Painswick and Windrush, has some fine 'wool' tombs in the churchyard) the road passes close to Broadwell Manor, built in 1757 as the home of the Hodges family, the then principal landowners here.

From Broadwell, minor roads lead east, to Evenlode (223291), and, after swinging north, to Chastleton (248292). The impressive house at Chastleton, an otherwise unremarkable village, dates from the early seventeenth century and largely retains its original form. The house, which is open to the public for part of the year, contains some fine furniture from the 1600s and a Bible reputedly gifted to Charles I before his execution. The small garden has topiary characteristic of the late seventeenth century.

Adlestrop (243270) has several eighteenth-century cottages but the village is chiefly of interest for Adlestrop Park, a house planned in the Gothic style about 1755 by a local man, Sanderson Miller. The house (and its gardens laid out by Humphrey Repton) is best seen from the footpaths leading across the parkland towards Daylesford (245269). Like Adlestrop, Daylesford has a number of attractive cottages but one larger building of importance: Daylesford House, to the east of the village in parkland. Daylesford House was built in 1787 for Warren Hastings. The architect was Samuel Pepys Cockerell, better known for his wonderful work in Indian and Muslim styles at Sezincote. Unlike Sezincote, however, the house at Daylesford has only a single dome derived from Muslim architecture, although there are further oriental features in interior decorations.

A little to the east, Cornwell (272272) has a lovely manor house overlooking intricate gardens and parkland. The house (in part), the gardens and much of the village itself are the work, in the early years of the twentieth century, of the architect Clough Williams Ellis, better known for the Italianate styling he brought to the creation of the Welsh village of Portmeirion.

The village of Oddington (230259), though attractive, is not particularly noteworthy but the lovely wall paintings in the church of St Nicholas should not be missed. The church stands isolated from the modern village down a lane to the south-east. The principal painting of interest here is the 'Doom' painting of the late fourteenth century. Look for the wonderful images represented in this Last Judgement: the dead being summoned from their graves, the damned being herded by devils into the mouth of Hell, repulsive monsters torturing sinners while the redeemed look on from the nearby heavenly city (which, since it is shown as a brick building, suggests the artist was not a local man). From Oddington, it is possible either to take the A436 and A44 toward Chipping Norton or, from the west end of the village, to follow the B4450 south down the Evenlode Valley.

This unusual picture of the Rollright Stones, taken during archaeological excavations in the 1940s, shows how much of the stones lie hidden beneath normal ground level.

Neither of the two small villages of Bledington (245228) or Kingham (260240) merits much attention, although St Leonard's Church at Bledington has some lovely architectural features, especially in the window tracery, and Kingham is prettily situated around a large village green. In nearby Churchill (282242) there is a massive local stone erected as a memorial to William Smith, the 'father of British geology', who was born here in 1769. This claim might be disputed by the likes of James Hutton and others, but Smith's work in mapping and stratigraphy was certainly crucial to the development of modern geology. It is no accident that the Cotswolds, and especially the area around Bath where Smith developed his ideas, should figure so largely in the history of geology. From Smith's monument, a narrow road leads north toward the earlier church here, now closed: on a house to the right, a brown plaque marks the birthplace, in 1732, of Warren Hastings. From Churchill, the B4450 will take you to Chipping Norton.

Chipping Norton (315271) is still an important market town but, like Cirencester, Northleach and Chipping Campden amongst others, no longer has the trade in wool and cloth that made it famous in the past. Unlike these towns, however, Chipping Norton is still a cloth manufacturing centre, if much reduced from former glories. Set in the valley to the south-west of the town and seen to advantage from both the B4450 and the A44 is the Bliss Valley Tweed Mill: a Lancashire factory built in 1872 with an Italianate chimney set in the Oxfordshire countryside!

The church, St Mary's, has elements of earlier work, but its principal feature is the nave, built about 1485 from monies gifted by John Ashfield, a local wool merchant. The tower is much later, dating from 1823. In 1549, the incumbent minister, the Rev. Henry Joyce, was charged with high treason and was hanged from the then tower for refusing to accept the new Prayer Book introduced by Edward VI. From the church, go uphill along Church Street past the row of almshouses built by 'Henry Cornish, gent. 1640', and into the wider spaces of Market Street. Several of the buildings here were re-faced or entirely rebuilt in the eighteenth century, testimony to the town's wealth and prosperity then, but this has had the effect of obscuring or entirely removing much of earlier interest. The Guildhall, for example, at the north end of Market Street, is sixteenth century in date, but later alterations hide its medieval features.

From Chipping Norton, head north. The B4026 and the minor roads through Over Norton will bring you to the villages of Great and Little Rollright and the Rollright Stones (which can also be reached via the A34(T) towards Stratford-upon-Avon). Alternatively, the A361 signposted to Banbury, will bring you to Hook Norton, Swerton, South Newington, and Bloxham and other places on the very edges of the Cotswolds.

Little Rollright (294302) is a tiny place and Great Rollright a mile or so to the east (325315) is not much bigger despite the name. Between the two villages and south of the road lies one of the most fascinating Bronze Age monuments in the whole country, the Rollright Stones (298308). The Stones are not all one set nor are they of the same date. The circle to the south of the road, the King's Men and the single King Stone in an enclosure to the north are contemporaneous at about 1500 or 2000BC; the nearby group called the Whispering Knights (down a lane south from the road) and earlier still, the remains of a Neolithic chambered long barrow now without its earth cover. Local folklore abounds with tales and traditions regarding the Rollright Stones: that they are the petrified figures of a forgotten king and his men, turned to stone by a local witch; that the King Stone will bleed if pricked at midnight; and that the stones in the circle cannot be counted (although seventy-seven seems to be the agreed number!). North-west of the Rollrights is the village of Hook Norton (355332), noted for its real ales. In Hook, as in many villages in the Oxfordshire wolds, the local stone is heavily iron-stained and the ironstone gives richer red-orange shades than in buildings further west and south. The church at Hook Norton, St Peter's, is surprisingly large for a village of this size. It has a lovely carved Norman font with representations of Adam and Eve and signs of the Zodiac. It is one of the finest in the Cotswolds and easily stands comparison with those at Southrop and Rendcomb. From Hook Norton, minor roads lead east through Wigginton toward the small town of Bloxham (430360) with the fourteenth-century spire of St Mary's visible for miles around. We are now, really, out of the Cotswolds. South here on the A361 will bring you back to Chipping Norton. But don't be in too great a hurry. Whether they lie in the Cotswolds or not, neither the medieval wall paintings in St Peter's Church, South Newington, nor the village of Great Tew a little to the south should be missed. In their own way, both are simply lovely.

The Cotswolds has many splendid church wall paintings (at Hailes, Baunton, and Oddington, for example), but few in the region or elsewhere can compare with those at South Newington (408333). The church, and most of the village, is set back off a bend in the main A361. What makes the paintings here so memorable is not so much the colour (and the fact that they have survived at all) as the vitality and detail of the figures shown: poor Thomas à Becket's head really is being split in two, and the martyrdom of Thomas of Lancaster, though less complete an image, is remarkable for the vigorous posture of the executioner as he strikes at the neck of the kneeling man. Other paintings include those of the Virgin and Child and one of St Margaret slaying a dragon. These and other paintings in the north aisle date from about 1340. As splendid in their own way, but in a very different style, are those on the north wall of the nave. These depict scenes from the Passion of our Lord, some very well preserved. These images are late fourteenth century and in a rustic and rather unsophisticated style.

South of South Newington and east off the B4022 (signposted from the A361) is the charming village of Great Tew (396294). The rustic and timeless charm of the place with its cottages of golden stone and thatched roofs set in a small valley is a deliberate creation, however. Although in origin earlier, the village is the result of early nineteenth-century estate rationalisation which, unlike most such 'improvements', included rather than removed the village. But it is easy to forget the harsh realities of life then or now as one strolls along the lanes here: chance survival or deliberate creation. Great Tew must epitomise for many (even if it is a false image) what the English country village looked like in the past.

From Great Tew, the B4022 and several minor roads lead south towards Wychwood Forest and the places of the same name, or the visitor can make for Chipping Norton and then south.

Wychwood Forest (335169) marks the eastern boundary of the Cotswolds. Its name is not derived from the 'wych' elm which used to form part of the forest, but from the Mercian tribe, the 'Hwicce', who ruled much of what is now the north Cotswolds in the seventh century. The Wychwood now is the remnant of a much larger forest once stretching from Burford to Woodstock. Although cleared in piecemeal fashion during the Middle Ages, it was still an extensive hunting forest of English royalty until the mid-1600s. Like the Forest of Dean, Wychwood was under the control of verderers and a forest ranger who, together with minor officers, controlled both the numbers of deer killed and managed the removal of trees. By the late eighteenth century, very little timber of quality remained, and from this period, clearance of the wooded areas for arable agriculture was rapid. The little hamlet of Field Assarts to the south of Leafield (319152) – itself dating from 1213 and clearance of the wood – testifies in its name to the continued removal of the forest cover (an 'assart' is a forest clearing).

Charlbury (360195) to the north-east of the Forest was once famous for its glove trade but is now a dormitory town for Oxford. Nearby, Cornbury Park (350180) has been the hunting

Great Tew village in a postcard view of c.1940.

lodge for Wychwood Forest since the time of Henry I although the present building dates from the mid-sixteenth century. Further east lie two attractive eighteenth-century houses and gardens: Ditchley Park (390210) and, near Woodstock, Blenheim Palace and Park (445160).

West of the Forest, Ascott-under-Wychwood (301189) lies on the south bank of the Evenlode. The remains of the early twelfth-century castle of one Ascott Doilly (and an earlier, un-dated, castle to the south-west of the present village), indicate the importance of the site as a river crossing. West along minor roads from here are Shipton-under-Wychwood (279179) and Milton-under-Wychwood (265182). Shipton is much the more interesting of the two villages and has some fine buildings. The Shaven Crown Inn, opposite the lane that leads down to St Mary's Church, is a fifteenth-century building, reputedly a guest house of nearby Bruern Abbey and now a sensitively-restored hotel and restaurant. Set back from a bend in the road is the splendid Jacobean Shipton Court, built about 1603. From here, the traveller can turn north and make for Stow-on-the-Wold, either through the small villages of Fifield, Idbury, and Westcote or through Bruern Abbey towards Bledington.

Nothing now remains of the foundation of St Mary-in-the-Heath (Bruern Abbey (269204) founded as a Cistercian house in 1147), save the faint outlines of medieval fishponds. Alternatively, go south from the Wychwoods towards Burford and the valley of the Windrush.

CHAPTER 13

Northleach, Burford and the Valley of the Windrush

Northleach (115146) lies in a hollow in the wolds about fourteen miles east of Cheltenham. It is a quiet attractive town, especially since the construction of the A40 bypass to the north, but long before then, Northleach's prosperity as a wool town had declined as the industry concentrated in the Stroud area. The market place's former role is reflected in its width. In the church of St Peter and St Paul behind the market place, the town's former involvement in the wool trade is evident in a splendid set of memorial brasses to local merchants.

St Peter's and St Paul's, like the churches at Chipping Campden, Burford, Fairford and Cirencester, is a 'wool' church. The south porch where one enters has fine medieval images: opposite the entrance door, look for the simple headstone (fourth from the path, on the left) to the poor unfortunate who 'died from the bite of a mad dog'. Inside, the earliest stonework is to be found in the chancel. The nave and clerestory were built from funds provided by John Fortey, wool merchant of Northleach who died in 1458. His memorial brass, showing him resting on a woolpack, is in the second bay of the nave. Permits to take brass rubbings from this and other brasses may be obtained from the Cotswold Pharmacy in the market place.

From the church, retrace your steps to the market place, turn left along the High Street, some of whose buildings have half-timbered upper storeys although most were re-faced in the eighteenth century, and make for the Cotswold Countryside Collection situated at the junction with the A429. The collections and displays of Cotswold rural life exhibited here are housed in the former Northleach House of Correction, built in 1798 by the prison reformer Sir George Onesiphorous Paul with the architect William Blackburn. The Northleach jail was built on a radial plan with the keeper's house (what is now the courtroom and tea-room) centrally positioned. The buildings were converted into a police station in 1857 and have been the Countryside Collection since 1980.

From here, an unsigned track leads across the fields to the nearby hamlet of Hampnett (the path begins on the right a little way up the hill on the old A40 road), or you can return to Northleach and visit the Harding's museum of mechanical music at the east end of the High Street. North of Hampnett and left off the A429 from Northleach, the three small villages of Turkdean (109175), Notgrove (109202) and Cold Aston (129199) – known also in the past as Aston Blank – stand exposed on the high wolds. Further east of these villages, and situated near the confluence of the south- and east-flowing Rivers Eye, Windrush, and Dikler, lies Bourton-on-the-Water (169208).

There has been a long history of settlement on or near the site of Bourton, chiefly as a result of its position as a crossing place on the Windrush. The town now straddles the river, several clapper bridges providing an attractive setting near the Green south of the High Street. Bourton has much to draw the visitor: a model village, a model railway, Birdland with its collections of exotic and not-so-exotic birds, a motor museum, and the Cotswold perfumery are among its attractions. And there are more gift 'shoppes' selling 'country fayre' than is credible (or tolerable) in a town of its size. There are some lovely buildings here – the late eighteenth early nineteenth-century church of St Lawrence, for example (positively modern as many Cotswold churches go). But don't expect to be alone when you visit Bourton. Like too many places, the town is being spoiled by the very things that feed it: the motor car, too many people, and a now sadly false projection of Cotswold 'charm'.

From Bourton, the River Windrush meanders south before turning eastwards just north of the village of Windrush (191132). There are several walks along this attractive valley, but the motorist has to follow minor roads along the valley sides. On the eastern side, minor roads from Bourton lead to the villages of Little Rissington (192198), and, further south, Great Rissington (199172). To the east of Little Rissington, the buildings of the RAF base sprawl across the hilltops, though the village itself with its isolated church to the north (St Peter's) has retained its character. Great Rissington centres around a rather untidy triangular green, with several of the most interesting buildings – the church, and a seventeenth-century manor house nearby (much restored in the 1920s) – tucked away in a corner of the village down narrow lanes from the road. The most attractive of the Rissingtons is Wyck Rissington (190215). The village is strung out along the road with many fine houses dating from the seventeenth and eighteenth centuries, set back from the village green. The church here, St Laurence's, has massively thick bases to the walls of the tower, a feature which has been taken to indicate construction in the twelfth century or perhaps even earlier. Inside there is beautiful fourteenth-century stained glass in the south window of the chancel – the positioning of the heavenly bodies is thought by some to have been influenced by a total eclipse of the sun in 1322 – and a collection of sixteenth-century Flemish carvings. Gustav Holst was organist here in 1892-93.

Although the main A40 road allows wider views of the valley of the Windrush, a quieter way to discover its delights is to take the minor road that runs south of the river before dividing to run on both banks east of the village of Windrush.

Many of the finest buildings in Sherborne (170148) hide behind the high walls of Sherborne Park, originally the home of the Dutton family who first built a house here toward the end of the sixteenth century. The Park divides the village in two, each of the west and east ends standing on small crossroads leading south to the A40. Continue eastwards from Sherborne towards Windrush (192131). The village is now spread along the roadside, although the old centre is around the small village green with St Peter's Church to the south-east. The churchyard has a number of good table-tombs, comparable with the best at Painswick, and the Norman south door of the church has a double row of beak-heads. The stone from the quarries and mines along the valley of the Windrush here was perhaps the best in the Cotswolds: the carving on monuments and the south doorway at St Peter's, Windrush, and the houses at nearby Great Barrington and Burford show how well it has been used.

From Windrush, the road runs east and divides just before Little Barrington (208128) with the left-hand fork crossing the

Windrush toward Barrington Park and Great Barrington (208137). Little Barrington, a little further on past the bridge, is attractively situated around a small stream and, in its own way, has a simple charm and dignity not matched by the grandeur of Barrington Park to the north.

Hidden behind high walls to the west of Great Barrington village – although the deer park and some buildings are visible through the wrought-iron gates as the road leaves the village to the north – Barrington Park was built in 1736, possibly by the architect and landscape gardener William Kent. The houses in Great Barrington (in truth, rather a sombre village) date from the seventeenth century but were much restored as part of overall estate improvements in the 1950s.

From the Barringtons, minor roads (the one south of the river gets very narrow in places) follow the river towards Burford. On the north side of the river, the small village of Taynton (232138) betrays now almost nothing of its past as a major centre for the working of local stone. Quarries at Taynton are recorded in Domesday Book, but are probably earlier than that by several centuries. They are now largely abandoned apart from small private workings. Stone from this little village was used for several Oxford colleges, notably All Souls and Christ Church, in Vanbrugh's Blenheim Palace near Woodstock, and for large parts of Wren's St Paul's in London.

From Taynton, the road to Burford (250122) joins the A424 north of the river, and, entering the town over the bridge of 1322, joins the south end of the High Street. Those coming to Burford from the south via the A40 or the A361 come downhill into the town, but have no less striking a first impression as a result. Certainly the church is best seen from north of the river.

There is much to discover in Burford. The town had a charter as early as 1087, and as it thrived as a market and centre of woollen manufacture in later centuries, so it expanded up the hill away from the river. The best place to start a walk around the town is the church of St John the Baptist (there's a car park a little to the east from the church, down Church Lane and across the river). Don't be in too great a hurry to enter the church. Near the church gate is a fine row of almshouses, founded in 1457 but restored several times

The memorial plaque to the Levellers on the north wall of St. John the Baptist's, Burford.

since, and on the wall of the church to the left of the south entrance porch a small plaque, erected by the Workers' Educational Association, commemorates three Levellers shot in the churchyard in May 1649. The Levellers were a group of radicals who believed that Cromwell was betraying the cause for which they had been fighting. A body of them were imprisoned in Burford in the church: one, Anthony Sedley, carved his name on the font, adding 'Prisoner'.

Once inside, the visitor is confronted by a complex plan and an architectural history which reflects the involvement of both town and church in the medieval wool trade. There is some evidence to suggest Saxon masonry here, but the present building is largely later twelfth-century in origin and late fifteenth-century in form. One of the most interesting features is much older still. In the south wall of the tower stair is a carving, probably dating from AD 100, showing the pagan goddess Epona, the Divine Horse, with two male supporters. The fact that Saxon builders often included such pagan objects in their own buildings may suggest that this tower is indeed Saxon in date. On the south transept side of the tower is a monument to Christopher Kempster, the local mason who worked with Sir Christopher Wren in late seventeenth-century London. As Kempster's memorial notes, 'He . . . was many Years employ'd in Building the Cathedral and Dome of St Pauls'.

As striking of its time as the pagan carvings in theirs is the monument erected in 1569, by one Edmund Harman, barber to Henry VIII. The North American natives shown here are said to be the earliest representations of Americans in Britain; the New World made 'real' for the citizens of sixteenth-century Burford. Other items of interest in the church include the ancient turret clock and the fine memorial tomb to Sir Lawrence Tanfield and his lady.

From the church, go down Lawrence Lane to the High Street. To the right and set back at right angles from the road is the line of Symon Wysdom's cottages, built in 1572. Wysdom was an important merchant and is said to have presented Elizabeth I with a bag of gold on the bridge when she visited Burford in 1574. From the cottages, make your way up the High Street again. On the right-hand side and on the corner with Priory Lane stands Falkland Hall, built in 1588 by Edmund Sylvester, a local wool and cloth merchant. Priory Lane leads, after two sharp corners, to Sheep Street. The Priory commemorated in the name was re-built as a private house in the later 1500s.

The Lamb Inn on the corner with Sheep Street dates in part from the fifteenth century. Close by, the local Tourist Information Office shares its premises with an off-licence selling wines and local real ales. On the south side of Sheep Street stand a number of town houses from the seventeenth century and earlier. Further out of town along Sheep Street – towards Upton on the B4425 – is the site of Kitt's Quarry, the source of Christopher Kempster's building stone. On the corner of Sheep Street and the High Street is the Tolsey Museum which has historical collections from all periods of Burford's past. From here, the view uphill is of terraced houses, some earlier than 1500 in origin if not in their frontage. Downhill, and toward the church, the scene is more crowded, and in some cases the buildings have not benefited from recent changes to their frontages.

South of Burford, the A361 leads to the Cotswold Wild Life Park (242083), and on to Lechlade. To continue along the valley of the Windrush, take either Witney Street (on the east side of the High Street) which connects with the A40 south of the river, or cross the bridge at Burford and turn right off the A361 in the village of Fulbrook. The small church here has several interesting features, but the village has been much restored. From Fulbrook, follow the minor road north of the Windrush toward Swinbrook (282122). This village was once the ancestral home of the Fettiplace family. Their house no longer survives, having been destroyed in 1806 (the only extant remains are included in the dairy in Pebble Court, south of the church), but their remarkable tombs in St Mary's Church testify to their former wealth. There are six Fettiplace effigies in total, reclining in groups of three on the north side of the chancel: compare the rigid stylisation of the Tudor figures with the more graceful lines of Stuart Fettiplaces. Outside, immediately to the west of the porch, are the graves of Nancy and Unity Mitford, as plain and unadorned as the Fettiplace monuments are ornate.

From the churchyard, a narrow lane runs at first between waist-high stone walls and then across fields towards the hamlet of Widford (271120), which may also be reached by a track from the Fulbrook road. Some of the bumps and hollows in the ground alongside the path from Swinbrook may be the remains of fishponds and formal terraces from the vanished Fettiplace house, and those around the small chapel of St Oswald's are certainly the house and field plans of the once more extensive, but now deserted, medieval village of Widford. The church here is remarkable for being built directly on the site of a Roman building. The remains of the Roman pavement, undiscovered until church restoration in 1904, can be seen on both sides of the chancel. The church also has fine medieval wall paintings and late eighteenth-century box pews: it should not be missed.

From Swinbrook, cross the river and turn left at the first junction toward Asthall (288113). The village stands on the route of Roman Akeman Street as it crosses the Windrush, and there was a Saxon river crossing here. The village is unremarkable, although it has a grand Elizabethan mansion house, once the home of the Redesdales. The church is of some interest, especially for its altar and other early medieval interior stonework. From Asthall, continue eastwards either by crossing the river here and taking the minor road through Asthall Leigh towards Minster Lovell or by joining the B4047 south of Asthall.

Minster Lovell (315110) is divided into two parts by the Windrush, the more modern town – 'New Minster' – lying south of the river. North of the river and right after the bridge, the road runs past an attractive row of cottages, some of Cotswold stone and slate and some with thatched roofs more typical of the West Midlands, towards Minster Lovell Hall (signposted from the B4047). The Hall ruins here are the remains of an early fifteenth-century manor house built by William Lovell. After being bought and partly dismantled by the Cokes, the Earls of Leicester, in the mid-eighteenth century, the house was left to decay. It is an impressive site, especially when seen from the open courtyard with the river to one's back. There was a small priory here, pre-dating the manor house, but no trace of it now survives. From the Hall, several footpaths lead off along the river banks: one leads back towards the bridge and the inn and makes an attractive perambulation of the village. St Kenelm's Church near the Hall has the alabaster tomb of William, Lord Lovell, the Hall's first owner.

From Minster Lovell, the B4047 leads east to the market town of Witney (355100). Witney has been a blanket-making town since the sixteenth century, and although the industry contracted after the 1914-1918 war, there are still three large mills active in the trade. There are several fine buildings in Witney, many fronting the market square at the south end of the High Street. The Buttercross here was originally a shrine: the worn steps are all that remain to indicate this earlier function. All around the market square, coaching inns and hotels like the Marlborough, the Crown Hotel, and the Angel reveal Witney's important role as an agricultural market as well as an industrial centre in the past. Church Green opens out south of the market square. The exterior of St Mary's is lovely, the interior a little bleak by the standards of some Cotswold churches. On the east side of the Green, look for 'The

The headstones to Nancy and Unity Mitford in Swinbrook churchyard.

Hermitage' and 'Wychwoods' as especially fine examples of seventeenth-century (and earlier) Cotswolds town architecture.

Just east of Witney (it may be reached via the A4095, Bridge Street and the B4022 from the town centre) is Cogges Manor Farm Museum. Cogges stands on the site of a deserted medieval village; only the church and priory and a later manor house survive. There is a history trail and a nature trail here and the Manor Farm is now a museum of farming and country life. During its open months (usually mid-March to early November) the museum hosts displays of country crafts and skills. The remains of the moated site here may be all that is left of the work of one Wadard, lord of the manor of Cogges in the late eleventh century. To the south, the River Windrush flows on in two separate channels before re-uniting with itself just north of its junction with the River Thames.

CHAPTER 14

Painswick, Bisley and the Slad Valley

There is a traditional rhyme in this part of the Cotswolds that runs:

> Mincing Hampton and Painswick Proud
> Beggarly Bisley and Strutting Stroud.

Bisley was certainly beggarly in the mid-1820s when a government report on the state of the woollen industry in the area noted that the town had over 2000 wholly unemployed persons in a total population of 6000. Painswick, also much involved with the cloth industry in the past, has had its shifts in fortune, but the town today is both proud of its past as a centre of wealth and is proudly situated on the western slopes of the Painswick Valley (865095), about six miles north of Stroud.

The area immediately around Painswick has been long settled: the Iron Age hillfort north of the town (868121) commands spectacular views over the scarp edge. Painswick itself is built of a paler stone than many villages in the Cotswolds and the result is a lovely freshness even though most of its buildings date from the seventeenth and eighteenth centuries or earlier. St Mary's church in the centre of the town was at the centre of fierce fighting in the Civil War. Cannon and bullet marks may still be seen on the west and east walls of the church. In Painswick, however, the church takes second place to the churchyard. Of the ninety-nine yews here, the oldest was planted in 1792: legend says a hundredeth will never grow. A 'Clipping Service' is held every year around the churchyard yews. This has nothing to do with shaping the trees but comes from an old meaning of clipping 'to embrace or encircle' (Old English *'clyppan'*). In the ceremony, village children join hands around the churchyard in celebration of the Church. The churchyard is also notable for its tombstones, some of the finest in England. Most of the tombs here, usually called table- or chest-tombs and sometimes in Painswick 'tea-

Parishioners encircle the church in the Painswick clipping ceremony. In 1897, the then vicar, Rev. Seddon, suggested in his work *Painswick Feast* that the ceremony was a direct descendant of the pagan Roman festival *Lupercalia*, which included 'animal sacrifice ... and scantily-clad youths rushing through the streets'. Nothing like that happens now!

caddies', commemorate local clothiers, wool merchants and others of wealth in some way connected with the town's past as a wool town. A Tomb Trail has been prepared; leaflets are obtainable from the church. The Packers, many of whose graves lie along the path leading from the north-east gate, were an important family in Painswick's cloth trade: 'Johannes Paccare' is recorded as a mercer in the town in the late fourteenth century. Hazelbury House, almost opposite the lychgate on the north side of New Street, was the home of Daniel Packer, a prominent clothier in Painswick who died in 1769. Both his house and his ornate gravestone are clear testimony to the prosperity of Painswick in the past. Other fine buildings along New Street include the Post Office, originally built in the fifteenth century and the only timber-framed building to survive in the town, and, at the corner with Bisley Street, the New Hall which was a clothmakers' hall as long ago as 1429.

From St Mary's Street to the south of the church, make your way down towards Painswick stream via Tibbiwell, Kemp's Lane leading into Knapp Lane, or even via Vicarage Street. Both Painswick Mill at the foot of Knapp Lane and Cap Mill further upstream were built in the seventeenth century. Savory's Pin Mill at the foot of Tibbiwell and Greenhouse Lane was used for cloth and corn as well as making pins. Other important mills in this early centre for non-factory-based industry (there were thirty-one mills on the Painswick stream and its tributaries at one time) include Salmon's Mill and the King's Mill downstream from the town and Loveday's Mill, used until c.1830, upstream towards the village of Sheepscombe (892102). This village, prettily situated at the head of Painswick Valley, was also dominated by cloth working in the past. One curate, coming to the village in the 1820s, observed of Wight's Mill there that 'the licentious ballad and the filthy jest and many an oath profane, were wont to echo within its walls'. The village is quieter today, to the outsider at least.

A little to the north of Painswick, clearly signposted from the town and well worth a visit is Painswick Rococo Garden (863105). The garden covers most of the ground north of Painswick House, built in the 1730s by Benjamin Hyett who also began the garden. The garden is still in the process of being restored, having lain as wilderness until clearance began in 1983 but there is much to delight the eye here. The garden is of interest for its combination of formal geometry such as the vista leading away from the Red House and the informality of its curving paths and architectural features in different styles. A copy of a painting of 1748 by the Gloucestershire artist Thomas Robins, who may also have designed the garden, hangs in the entrance to the garden. This painting is of particular interest for two reasons. There is some doubt that certain parts shown were actually built, and in this sense the view is of a garden perhaps more imagined than real. Further, it is an ectopic picture, the perspective shown of the garden is impossible to achieve from this (or any) position, leave alone from the point where Robins himself drew it (he is shown in the left corner of the painting, seated near the Pigeon House).

From Painswick, take the minor road down Tibbiwell Lane

Bisley Street, Painswick, c.1910. The White Horse Inn on the left is now a bookshop but otherwise the view has hardly changed.

and up Greenhouse Lane on the eastern side of the valley towards Bull's Cross (877087). There are wonderful views down the Painswick and Slad valleys here and several footpaths leading off.

Slad village (872074) and the Slad Valley have been made famous through Laurie Lee's *Cider with Rosie*, a vivid account of a Cotswold childhood between the wars. Like the neighbouring valley villages, Slad was once involved in cloth manufacture. Steanbridge, at the crossing of the Slad Brook, had a working mill until 1825; it figures at the squire's house in Lee's novel. From Slad, a minor road signposted to Elcombe (in places little more than a lane) leaves the B4070 and climbs the eastern slopes of the Slad Valley past Swift's Hill (877067) and Elcombe (882070) towards Bisley and the Toadsmoor Valley. From the top of Swift's Hill, it is possible to look down the valley beyond Stroud and follow the scarp edge as it curves and dips away to the south-west. The lane past Swift's Hill towards Catswood Farm and Bisley is so deep-set in the scarp edge and so overhung with trees that it is like passing through a tunnel to reach the downland at the top.

A right turn at the crossroads at Stancombe Farm (898069) will take you towards the Lypiatts. About half a mile along this road, the square shaft and base-member of a now headless Saxon cross of about AD 700 may be seen in a small fenced enclosure to the left. Lypiatt Park (886059) is a late fourteenth-century building much altered in the early 1880s. It is not open to the public although glimpses of the house may be seen from the road. Middle Lypiatt (878047) has a fine Tudor house; Nether Lypiatt further to the south is a manor house from the early eighteenth century.

Bisley (903060) may be reached by crossing the minor road, the Calf Way, at Stancombe Farm. Beggarly in the early nineteenth century it may have been, but Bisley today has a quiet prosperity and charm. Most of the buildings in the High Street date from the seventeenth century. The Bear Inn, at the top of George Street and past the two-celled village lock-up dated 1824, used to be the village court house. The church, All Saints, was the charge of Thomas Keble, John's brother, from 1827 to 1873. Keble was responsible for the restoration of the church in 1862 and for the institution in 1863 of the annual Well-Dressing ceremony in Bisley, held at the five gabled wells south of the church. The interior of the church contains some fine early stone coffin lids of the eleventh and twelfth centuries together with the tomb-chest of a thirteenth-century knight. The church's finest treasure is outside in the churchyard: the 'rocket-shaped' poor soul's light, dating from the later 1200s, and used for candles for masses to be said for the poor. It is the only one out-of-doors in England.

Minor roads south from Bisley lead to Eastcombe, Chalford, Oakridge and villages along the valley of the River Frome. If heading north from Bisley, a minor road running north-eastwards leads through Calfway Farm towards Througham. This farm was once the site of a calf enclosure, a 'calf-haga', in Old English, and the name has at some later time been applied to the minor road east of Stancombe Farm. The road through Calfway Farm is very steep in places: not suited to caravans at any time and difficult for cars in winter. From the top of the rise north of the farm, a lane leads eastward to Througham Slad (926065), a small hamlet chiefly of note for the fine seventeenth-century house there restored by Jewson in 1931. A footpath leads east through the woods towards Edgeworth (945060). The village here has several good farm buildings,

The '2-berth' village lock-up in Bisley: proof, perhaps, of a lower crime rate in the past.

and the church, St Mary's, still shows something of its Saxon beginnings as well as an attractive Perpendicular west tower.

North of Througham Slad and set back from the road is Througham (921079), which has a lovely early seventeenth-century gabled house restored in the 1930s and again in the late 1980s. The Camp (913093) is a hamlet with several good cottages and farm buildings and a short way further north, the right-hand road at the crossroads leads through Wishanger and towards the village of Miserden.

Miserden (938091) is a pleasant village whose attractive situation affords fine views, especially north-eastwards across the steeply-wooded slopes of the Frome Valley towards Caudle Green and Syde. The church was violently over-restored in the nineteenth century and lost much of its architectural interest then, although some Saxon remains survive. In the south chancel chapel there is a very fine tomb-chest of Sir William Sandys, who died in 1640. In the churchyard is the simpler memorial to a Miserden shepherd, one Samuel Hurrell, who died in 1807: 'From Youth through life, the Sheep was all his care'. Miserden Park mansion to the east end of the village is Elizabethan in origin, with more recent additions to house and garden by Lutyens. There is a garden centre here with a good selection of plants and shrubs. In private woods to the east lie the remains of the motte and bailey of the Musard family, the Norman landlords from whom the village takes its name.

North of Miserden are several interesting villages. Both Caudle Green (945105), a hamlet with a large green and good views, and Winstone (961095), may be walked to from Miserden through woods along the Frome Valley, some of which are used for pheasant hatcheries. Caudle Green is a good centre for local walks and it is only a short way east across the valley to the hamlet of Syde (949109). The church here, St Mary's, has lovely seventeenth-century box pews. Nearby is a large tithe barn. If you go by car, the villages of Winstone, Caudle Green and Syde may be reached from Miserden by taking the lane south via Parson's Hill (949080) and joining the minor road west of Duntisbourne Abbots.

North-west of Miserden is the small, and in Cotswold terms very modern, village of Whiteway (918103), which was founded in 1898 by the Brotherhood Church of Croydon, a socialist-humanist society much influenced by Tolstoyan ideas: to hold everything in common, without the need of money, and without formal government. Initial attempts at running the settlement on these principles were unsuccessful and by the early 1900s, families had turned to domestic and small-scale manufactures such as baking and leathercraft in order to make ends meet. Their housing is today subject to local planning restrictions, but despite this and other ways in which the original intentions have not been fully realised, the colonists of Whiteway still hold their land in common, and many other aspects of their communitarian principles still flourish.

Brimpsfield (940127) is older than Whiteway by at least 900 years, and for such a small village has much of interest. The manor was held in Saxon times by a thegn named Duns, but was granted by William the Conqueror to the Giffards. The motte and bailey remains of the earliest castle lie to the foot of the slopes east of the village near Brimpsfield Park. The rather more extensive remains of a later Giffard castle, pulled down in 1322 after the family rebelled against Edward II, are situated just south of the church. The masonry was used for buildings in the village: Brimpsfield House, although largely seventeenth century, has stonework from the castle built into its roof and walls.

Brimpsfield's church, St Michael's, is early Norman and was almost certainly built by a Giffard. The nave has a well-preserved roof of ancient timbers and other interesting features include medieval tombstones, perhaps commemorating the Giffards, of the fourteenth century or earlier. A Priory once stood near the church. There is no trace of it today except that incorporated in a large stone-built chicken shed in a field to the west end of the church are some stones and arched window surrounds said to be from the Priory.

The village is one of the highest in the Cotswolds, and from the eastern end of the rise on which the church stands, the sweeping views eastwards include the line of the Roman Ermin Way, now the A417, as it runs with an almost unbending directness between Birdlip and Cirencester, the site of Roman Corinium.

CHAPTER 15

Stroud, Nailsworth and the Cotswold Woollen Towns

It has been said of Stroud that the town '. . . holds naught that's pretty, wise or witty'. Neither this nor the epithet 'strutting' is deserved, although it is true that the town's former rôle as the centre of the Cotswolds woollen industry has left it and surrounding valleys an industrial legacy neither typical of the area as a whole nor always attractive. But much of what does remain of this past is of great interest and historical importance. And in the rolling commons between the steep-sided valleys, in the views from these and the scarp edge near places like Coaley Peak, and in its many buildings and smaller villages, the Stroud district offers a great deal to discover in a small area. Given Stroud's position, it is possible to explore away from the town along each of the cardinal directions: north to Painswick or Slad, west and east along the valley of the Frome and each of the villages between Stonehouse and Chalford, and south towards Nailsworth.

Stroud (852051) lacks the character of many Cotswold towns but has several buildings of interest. The Subscription Rooms on the north side of George Street, built in 1833 in the neo-classical style, are one of the town's finest buildings and, since the Tourist Information Office is housed here, they make a good place to begin a walk. Next door, and complementing the Subscription Rooms in style and date, is the Congregational Chapel. From the square, go uphill along Kendrick Street and into the High Street. This street and the several roads leading from it – The ˍShambles, Union Street, Church Street – represent the core of medieval Stroud. The Town Hall, built in 1594, is the only building of this period to survive in the town, and even it has some Victorian additions. Rather than go back to the High Street, continue along the Shambles into the yard of St Lawrence's Church. The church was almost entirely rebuilt in the late 1860s, although the tower is original and dates from the fourteenth century. From the church, make your way through Bank Gardens, and, before coming out into

Lansdown, turn right up a short flight of stairs into the small display of Stroud's industrial past laid out in an annexe to the main museum. Though small, the exhibition here is well presented: there is a handloom (though a later model than those used by most domestic weavers in the area), and a display of local trades and industries including examples of fine broadcloth.

The major part of Stroud Museum is housed in the former School of Science and Art in Lansdown (to the right as you come out of the industrial display). The material here is not presented half as well as in the annexe, a pity since there is a lot to interest amongst the local archaeological finds, and the painting of the red and blue cloths drying on tenter hooks gives a wonderful impression of the colour and scale of the wool industry in the past. From the Museum, retrace your steps along Lansdown to the junction with Gloucester Street. A right turn here down Gloucester Street will take you past the former police station and, if you cross over Slad Road and go up Beeches Green, will bring you to Stratford Park Leisure Centre. (Beeches Green, Gloucester Street, and the most inappropriately-named Merrywalks here are all major roads, so getting to Stratford Park is actually easier and more pleasant by car.) Both Stratford Lodge and the attractive iron bridge here date from the early nineteenth century. The Leisure Centre has outdoor and indoor swimming pools as well as other recreational facilities including squash courts and a sauna. King Street, the continuation of Lansdown, is much spoilt by modern developments. From King Street, either of George Street or Russell Street to the left will bring you back to the Subscription Rooms.

The growth of Stroud along the river valleys has rather obscured the boundaries of the smaller villages in the area, yet places like Dudbridge, Cainscross, and Ebley still retain something of their own identity within this shared industrial past. One important link between these places in the past was the canal, the Stroudwater Navigation which joined the area with midland England via the Severn. Parts of the canal are now again navigable and walking the towpath is a quieter and better way to discover than motoring. Several cycle routes are clearly indicated and it is possible to do a circular cycle route via Woodchester.

From the Bath Road (the A46), a path leads down and along the Frome Valley. The walk is an industrial archaeologist's dream come true. Lodgemoor Mill (which may also be reached via the A4096 Cainscross-Stonehouse road from Stroud) is one of the few working mills in the area. Run by Messrs. Winterbottom, Strachan and Playne who manufacture cloth for billiard tables, uniforms, and tennis ball covers as well as for Vatican robes, the present mill, built in 1875 (the clothier's house from the early eighteenth century still survives), occupies a site known to have been used in cloth making for at least 700 years. From the mill, go past the mill pond and over the bridge to Fromehall Mill and continue along the towpath towards Dudbridge.

The present Redlers buildings at Dudbridge are in places eighteenth century but are mostly nineteenth century and the site of the once major firm of Apperley, Curtis and Co. which closed in 1933. From Dudbridge, the B4066 leads south towards the village of Selsey (833039), home of one of the great Stroudwater mill-owning families in the past, the Marlings. To continue along the valley, either turn right off the Selsey road down Meadow Lane or take the first turn right to cross the canal and rejoin the towpath. Both routes bring you to Ebley Mill, built in 1818 and owned by the Marlings. The greater part of the mill which, no longer working, has been converted to house Stroud District Council Offices, was based upon the earlier Ebley Court, built in 1587. The six-storey mill tower with its steep slate roof has a companion piece in the tower of All Saints Church in Selsey. This was built, as was the factory tower, by G. F. Bodley in 1862 under the direction of Sir Samuel Stephens Marling who is said to have followed the style of a church at Marling in the Austrian Alps. The church has what is widely regarded as the earliest ecclesiastical stained glass produced by William Morris, or, more properly, by his devotees, since there is work here by Ford Maddox Brown and Sir Edward Burne-Jones. In its construction and embellishments with money gained from industry, Selsey church can claim to be a wool church in just the same way as those of Northleach, Fairford, or Chipping Campden.

Further west along the Frome Valley is Kings Stanley Mill. Also at one time owned by the Marlings, this is one of the most remarkable buildings of the industrial revolution. It was constructed entirely without wooden materials. The L-shaped five-storey building was built between 1812 and 1813: the latter date is evident in several places on the ironwork including the ornate fanlights. If, as seems to be generally agreed, the mill was the first fireproof industrial building in England, it is also true that it was not the only such construction since naval dockyards of the early 1800s display similar features. What is also remarkable about this building of cast-iron beams and stone flag floors is that it is still not known who designed it.

North of the river and canal, the small town of Stonehouse (809052) sits where the Frome Valley meets the Severn Vale. In the early nineteenth century, Stonehouse had some pretensions to being a Cotswold spa, but never achieved anything like the popularity of Cheltenham or Bath. Like many such places on the scarp-vale borders, the town lacks that unity of style that comes from use of local stone in building, but in the setting of St Cyr's Church, off Church Lane from the A419 Bristol Road, Stonehouse has a feature to rival many things in the Cotswolds proper. Above the town on the scarp edge the village of Randwick (830067) has revived the Randwick Wap, an annual fair which used to be organised by local weavers but which was suppressed because of the fighting and drunkenness that accompanied it. The Wap, held now in May, was one of several such events in this part of the Cotswolds. Others like the Nympsfield Revels and the Coaley Wake held in the past near Easter have not been revived. From Randwick which, via émigré weavers in the 1840s, gave its name to Randwick in New South Wales, a minor road leads to the small villages of Ruscombe and Whiteshill, both former weaving villages also brought to a state of great destitution by the collapse of the industry. From Whiteshill, the road goes north towards Pitchcombe and Painswick or south to Stroud via Puckshole and Paganhill. The arch at Paganhill was erected to commemorate Wilberforce's Emancipation Act of 1833 which effectively ended slavery in the British colonies. It once stood as the entrance to estate land; its position now on the edge of a housing estate is a little incongruous.

East of Stroud, the River Frome again runs alongside a canal, the Thames and Severn, and the combination of both with the small villages and mills in the steep-sided valley known as the Golden Valley is delightful. The industrial past of places like Bowbridge, Thrupp, and Brimscombe is less evidently a woollen past than in other villages in the area since many mills and factories have been much altered in their conversion to alternative uses. It was a Brimscombe man, Joseph Lewis, who in 1815 invented the rotary cutter to replace the cumbersome manual shears until then used in cutting cloths. The idea of a rotating drum on which angled blades moved across a surface and cut off raised material as they went was later adapted by another local man, Edwin Budding, as the basis to the modern lawnmower. The display of industrial machinery in the annexe to the Stroud Museum has a cross-cutting machine, the Museum has an early lawnmower, and it is easy to see the links in design between the two.

The village of Chalford (900025) is situated on the steep north slopes of the Golden Valley, so steep in places that many roads are unsuitable for motor traffic. A good starting point for a walk around this attractive village is to turn right off the A419 at Belvedere Mill, down an unsignposted road. Belvedere Mill stands together with a lengthsman's house, a round building close to the canal, and several former weavers' cottages as well as a clothier's house in a very pleasing setting. A lengthsman was someone in charge of a given length of the canal. From this position (car parking is possible close to the wall as the road goes over the river), walk along the minor road towards the large buildings of St Mary's Mill. The first building on the right here was once the Company's Arms Inn, where buyers from the East India Company and other firms came to deal: opposite are weavers' cottages. Near the entrance to St Mary's Mill, turn toward the railway line and take the narrow footpath (often muddy even in good weather) that runs along the back of the mill behind a wall. The mill was built in about 1820, although the mill house is earlier. Though it is not as imposing as Ebley, Kings Stanley Mill or the Dunkirk Mill at Nailsworth, looking at St Mary's Mill from this vantage point gives a good impression of how crowded industrial development was along the valley floors. Continue along this path to cross over the A419 as the main road rises out of the valley floor and continue along the canal towpath. The Thames

This early photograph (c.1860) of Rack Hill, Chalford, shows the cloth racks on the far side of the valley, the railway in the foreground.

and Severn Canal was begun in 1783 to connect the Stroudwater Navigation with the London Basin system via Stroud and Lechlade. The canal, now partly filled, runs parallel with the River Frome along the valley east of Chalford towards Frampton Mansell before disappearing into the tunnel just east of Daneway near Sapperton (946033). The towpath walk here is quiet and full of interest: the canal bridges still show their dates of construction, the canal is now the haven for all sorts of wild life and flowers, and on the slopes, small cottages and houses occupy the former sites of the tenter racks used for drying cloths.

Above Chalford on the northern slopes of the Golden Valley, the villages of Brownshill (886025), Oakridge (915035), and Far Oakridge (926036) are situated on the edge of the wolds on what, until the late 1860s, was common land and part of the parish of Bisley. The quiet charm of these places, and of Eastcombe (891044), a little further north on the edge of the attractive Toadsmoor Valley, belies the major impact the enclosure of these common lands had upon the people at the time.

South of the Golden Valley, the minor road which crosses both canal and river at Belvedere's Mill in Chalford leads uphill through Hyde towards the high wolds villages of Avening and Minchinhampton. The road south from Hampton Fields (885997) passes Gatcombe Park, once the home of David Ricardo the political economist, from whose ownership in the 1820s the present house dates. Gatcombe Park, now the home of HRH Princess Anne, had originally been built in 1770 for the local industrial family, the Sheppards of Uley. Avening (883979) was once a cloth-making town, but never on a par with the larger centres to the west. The Church of the Holy Cross here, attractively situated off a bend in the road and near the stream, has a scarlet cloth on display as witness to its past prosperity. From here, the A434 leads to Tetbury or north through wooded valleys to Nailsworth. A right turn off this road (opposite the Weighbridge Inn) will bring you to Minchinhampton (which can be reached more directly by turning right at the crossroads south of Hyde when coming from the Golden Valley).

Minchinhampton (872007), which has the unusual distinction for Cotswolds villages of being twinned with a Tanzanian village, Nkokoto, has in recent years sprawled westwards out across the downs. The old core of the village, centred around the Market House built in 1698, the High Street, and the twelfth-century Church of the Holy Trinity, is much less spoilt. There are attractive buildings and quiet little streets off the market place, especially to the south and east, but the thing to see has to be the stained glass in the church's south transept window. If you come to the church from the market place, go up the stone-flagged path past the cottages and you will pass the window on the outside before entering. Its beauty is best appreciated from within, with, if possible, bright sunlight streaming in from outside. It is a lovely feature, quite the rival of many other Cotswolds stained-glass windows.

North of the village proper, Minchinhampton Common has remarkably well-preserved Iron Age earthworks, the Bulwarks, running roughly north-east to south-west across land now open to grazing horses and also used as a golf course. In part, the Bulwarks enclose the Iron-Age hillfort known as Amperley Camp. At the crossroads just past the earthwork, six roads run

The teazle tower near Frogmarsh Mill, Woodchester.

across the commons. Continuing straight on will bring you to the next area of common land, Rodborough Common, which, like Minchinhampton, has wonderful views from the edge. For the more adventuresome, a slower but much more attractive way of getting to Rodborough Common is by way of the tiny hamlet of St Chloe, tucked under the lip of the hill; then follow the narrow lane as it curves around the edge above the Woodchester Valley. At the edge of the Common, the castle-like building is Rodborough Fort, known locally as 'the Folly' and built in 1761, although the present building dates only from 1870. It is now part of a caravan and campsite. The identity of Rodborough itself has been rather lost in the growth of Stroud, although there is an attractive grouping of cottages as the road narrows coming down from the Common.

From Rodborough, follow the A434 towards Nailsworth. It is worth making a slight detour to go through the village of Woodchester (842025). Woodchester Mill, sited near the junction of the main road and the minor road over the Nailsworth Stream, is today a piano factory. In 1788, when George III visited the mill, it was part of an industrial and commercial complex owned by the Paul family, one of whose descendants, Sir George Onesiphorous Paul left industrial management for a life in politics. (In the Cotswolds, his work as a prison reformer has left us the jails at Gloucester and Northleach). From Woodchester Mill, a cycle path keeps closer to the stream than to the road. Walking or driving through Woodchester itself will bring you to Churches Mill, built in the early seventeenth century as a corn and fulling mill and now producing walking sticks, and, from there via the cycle path and a short stretch alongside the main road, to the attractive group of buildings around Frogmarsh Mill. The round tower here is thought to have been used for storing teazles, widely used to raise the nap on cloths. From here, go past the mill and take the footpath to join the High Street through Woodchester and thence back to the starting point near Woodchester Mill.

In addition to these industrial buildings, Woodchester has some interesting nineteenth-century architecture, particularly in St Mary's Church designed by S. S. Teulon in 1863, in the house at Woodchester Park, set within a valley to the west of the village, and designed in part at least by Pugin, and in the Dominican Priory. The village is also notable for what cannot be seen, in the original at least, for in the grounds of the old church of St Mary abandoned in the same year Teulon was building the new St Mary's, there lies one of the finest of all Roman tesselated pavements. Woodchester villa was first uncovered by the late eighteenth-century archaeologist, Samuel Lysons, whose *An Account of the Roman Antiquities discovered at Woodchester in the County of Gloucester* (1797) was a model scientific report by the standards of the day, even if it was not a complete guide. Lysons never found the bath suite in his excavation of the sixty-four rooms he did find, and contemporary archaeologists think there is more to be found still. The prize feature of the Woodchester villa is the Orpheus pavement, most probably constructed by paviours of the Cirencester (Corinium) school, in which the central figure is surrounded by wild animals in a variety of animated poses, as he plays music to lament the death of his wife, Eurydice. All of this is merely infuriating to know, of course, since the mosaic and villa are buried: the Orpheus pavement used to be exposed every ten years by Woodchester locals but this no longer happens. (A small compensation is the reproduction of the pavement in the Tabernacle building in Wotton-under-Edge.)

If governments can find millions of pounds for aircraft whose roars disturb the Cotswold scene, you would think they could find enough to uncover and display one of the most important Roman monuments in northern Europe.

Much of Nailsworth (850995) lies off the main roads that run through the town. There are some pleasant buildings here, even if modern developments have not always been sympathetic to the character of the place. The road from Woodchester comes into Nailsworth past the Dunkirk Mills, whose present buildings date to about 1820 but which, from the spring of 1989, have been converted to what estate agents call 'Quality Apartments and Penthouse suites on a Riverside setting'. Times change. This mill was once one of the largest buildings in the Stroudwater woollen industry, and part of a complex which included Egypt Mill nearer Nailsworth (itself now a bar and restaurant where the water wheel and gearing systems have been restored as working features). Near the crossroads in the centre of town, plans by speculators to demolish the George Hotel and 'develop' the site have brought into sharp focus the issue of restoration and conversion of old buildings to modern use.

From the crossroads near the clock tower, the minor road which curves up the hill towards the hamlet of Watledge (and from there to Minchinhampton) is fronted by several attractive buildings. The row of cottages on the left here near the stream is very pleasing. The houses which line the main A46 as it runs uphill and out of the town towards Bath and the south Cotswolds are mostly undistinguished and the centre of town has been overly responsive to the needs of the motor car. But in places along the B4058, and in the upper town to the west, there are a number of interesting seventeenth- and eighteenth-century cottages.

From Nailsworth, the A434 winds through the valley towards Avening. Longford Mill on this road, down to the left just after the sign to Minchinhampton, was certainly in operation in 1705 and is still a working concern producing tennis ball cloth. The mixture here of stately clothier's house, early mill buildings of local stone and later brick development, all in various states of repair, gives a good idea of the fluctuating fortunes of the industry. And on calm and warm days when the weaving shed doors are open for air, the sounds are evocative, too.

South from Nailsworth, the village of Horsley (840980) deserves more than to be driven through at speed. In the valley here, commercial trout farming has developed on the site of cloth-drying and bleaching fields; the narrow and steep road through the tiny hamlet of Washpool will bring you down to the valley floor from Horsley (and out on to the A46). Horsley once had a major priory and a prison designed by Onesipherous Paul. Nothing survives of the first nor above ground of the second although foundations of the prison are now supporting at least one house here. From Horsley, take the B4058 towards Wotton-under-Edge but, about half a mile before joining with the A4135, turn right and downhill towards the village of Uley. The minor road to the left before the turn is signposted to Kingscote, the important Roman site and now a tiny village (819962) whose lords of the manor lived here, generation upon generation, from the early twelfth century until 1956: continuity with change – like the Cotswolds as a whole.

The countryside between Stinchcombe Hill (740986) and Dursley (758980) to the south and west and the villages of Uley (789982) and Nympsfield (802003) to the east and north is delightful. There are lovely views of Uley and the small village of Owlpen down this minor road from the B4058. Alternatively, continuing on via the A4135 will bring you more directly to Dursley. From there and the walks on Stinchcombe Hill, you can follow the route below in reverse order.

The minor road enters Uley from the south-east past a scattering of pleasing cottages and houses although the larger building on the rise to the left, Stout's Hill, once the home of Gloucestershire's county historian, Samuel Rudder, has not been well served by its change of identity to a time-share property. From the junction here, turn right into Uley itself. Once a cloth-making town of some importance (the first to make Spanish cloth in the Cotswolds), Uley is now a quiet place and a good centre from which to walk to the several points of interest nearby. Uley Bury fort, set on the edge of the wolds to the north of Uley, is at about thirty-two acres one of the largest Iron Age hillforts in Britain. The views from here are wonderful and although the interior cannot be viewed, there is a walk around the perimeter. From Uley, the walk goes left off the B4066 just before the village of Crawley (left through a mesh netting gate as the minor road divides from a track to the right). The walk around Uley Bury will bring you back to your starting point, but there are longer walks along the scarp from this point that lead either out to the more isolated hills of Cam Long Down and Peaked Down, or you can follow the edge along towards Coaley Peak and Frocester Hill. Alternatively, drive to Coaley Peak Picnic Site further north on the B4066 and take your choice of the several walks that lead off from here. From the hill here, the remains of former field systems and strip lynchets on the edge of Cam Long Down can be clearly seen; and beyond, the Tyndale Monument, Stinchcombe Hill and the sweeping curves of the River Severn. In the Picnic Site, the remains of the Coaley Peak or Nympsfield Long Barrow have been partially restored in 1974, after the third of three major excavations. This ancient monument is rather outshone by the wonderfully-named long barrow, Hetty Pegler's Tump. Signposted from Uley, the grassed-over mound can be visited down a path from the road: keys to the chamber are available nearby. The monument takes its name from a certain Hester Pegler who owned the land in the seventeenth century.

From the village green in Uley, the narrow road right after the Old Crown Inn leads down a steep hill to Owlpen Manor and the Church of the Holy Cross. The manor house is in a lovely quiet setting with a stream and a small terraced garden to the south-facing front. It is essentially a late medieval building but with important additions from the eighteenth century and the late 1920s. In the grounds nearby, a corn mill has been well restored. Both the manor (in part) and cottages here are available for country holiday accommodation.

Dursley is sheltered from the west by the wooded slopes of Stinchcombe Hill. Lanes from the town are signposted to the hill and, in addition to the golf course here, there are several circular walks across Stinchcombe Common and around the wooded edge of the hill. After Stroud, Dursley is the largest town in the district and, like its larger neighbour, is now reliant upon modern industries, especially the firms of Listers and Mawdsleys to replace past involvement with cloth production. Unthinking recent developments have not always helped the town retain its character, but there are some fine buildings in Long Street, which runs off at an angle from the impressive Market House built in 1738. At the end of Long Street is the house known as The Priory, built by Edward Webb, a local clothier, in about 1540 (above the doorway, the initials E W and the date 1520 are still just visible). A right turn at the bottom of Long Street near the River Ewelme and then right again past old mill buildings into Water Street will bring you back near the Market House.

From Dursley, minor roads through the villages of Cam, Lower Cam, Hamshill and Coaley lead across the vales with the Cotswolds edge to the east. The village of Frocester can either be reached in this way or by turning down the hill near where the road east leads to Nympsfield. Frocester (785033) is worth spending some time in, even for such a small place. Aside from its important Roman villa (excavated but not visible to the public), there is a magnificent tithe barn of thirteen bays, built about 1300 on estates owned by the abbots of Gloucester. The Frocester Court barn is part of a larger complex of important historic farm buildings including the manor house itself and a seventeenth-century lambing pen. From the Frocester Hill road (itself Roman) turn right in the village towards Leonard Stanley (802033). Like Frocester, this is worth a visit for its farm buildings. Stop near the Church of St Leonard's, which has a very fine nave roof dating from the fourteenth century, and, on coming out of the church, go down the path leading more or less straight from the porch door to the corner of the churchyard nearest the farm entrance. Turn into the farm. Just past farm buildings on the left that bear the date 1848 above the byre doors, there is a small building set at right angles to the lane. Look at the masonry to the left of the front wall. This 'herring-bone' pattern is characteristic of Anglo-Saxon masonry: what is now a farm outhouse was once an Anglo-Saxon chapel, probably late eleventh century. This chapel, the tithe barn and other buildings here are the remains of a priory established in Leonard Stanley in about 1120. The large farmhouse is called Priory Farmhouse, and, if you look carefully at the window surrounds in the barn and the chapel, the remains of medieval windows become evident.

From Leonard Stanley, the road north across the Frome leads to Stonehouse. Go east and, via Kings Stanley and Selsey, the road returns you to Stroud.

CHAPTER 16

Cirencester, Capital of the Cotswolds

Cirencester today is a thriving market town drawing custom from all over Gloucestershire and beyond. It is a function the town has fulfilled since the Roman period at least. Roman Cirencester, *Corinium Dobunnorum* (usually abbreviated to Corinium), was the second most important town of Roman Britain. Pre-Roman settlement in the area centred not upon what is now Cirencester, however, but on the Iron-Age town of Bagendon, the capital or 'oppidum' of the Dobunni tribe from whom the Roman town took its name. Parts of the earthwork remains of Bagendon may still be seen on both sides of the minor road running north from Perrot's Brook (017065), about three miles north of Cirencester on the A435. In Cirencester itself, much more survives of the Roman town, and from later periods, to strengthen the town's claim that today, and more especially in the past, it was and is the 'capital' of the Cotswolds.

The Romans occupied Cirencester for nearly 350 years, from about AD 60 to the withdrawal of official Roman civic authority in AD 410. The form of their town has influenced later building ever since. The Saxons built a church here, in its day the longest in England, on the same site as the later Augustinian Abbey founded in 1117 and demolished in 1539. The present parish church of St John the Baptist is one of the largest in England and is, in the words of one eighteenth-century historian, a 'magnificent and sumptuous building'. All around the town are fine examples of seventeenth- and eighteenth-century buildings put to modern use. Medieval buildings survive in the Weavers' Hall, in St. John's Hospital and in the Norman gatehouse, the only surviving remains of the once extensive Abbey. And in Cirencester Park, the town possesses one of the finest early landscape gardens in Britain. With so much to discover and to interest, a walk around the town is the best way to explore, and the parish church in the market place is a good place to start. Maps of the town may be purchased from local newsagents or the Tourist Information Office.

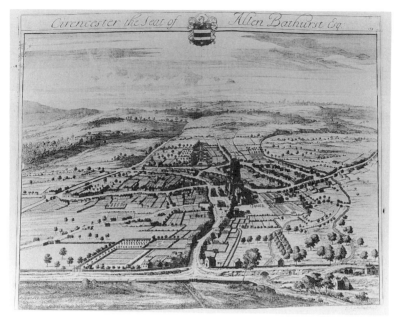

Cirencester in the early eighteenth century, from an engraving by Kip, c.1709, in Atkyns' *The Ancient and Present State of Glocestershire*, second edition 1768.

The earliest church on the site of the present-day St John the Baptist's was built about 1120, contemporary in fact with the foundation of the Augustinian Abbey in the town. Little remains of this first Norman church. What stands today is the result of successive alterations from the twelfth and thirteenth centuries with the majestic tower, a relatively early example of the Perpendicular style, dating from the early 1400s. The tower was financed through a gift to the Abbey and the town after the townsfolk had apprehended (and later beheaded) two leaders, the Earls of Kent and Salisbury, of the rebellion against Henry IV. Don't be in too great a hurry to view the interior: the three-storey south porch, built about 1490, is magnificent with its canted oriel windows and fan-vaulting.

Of the church's five chapels, the Trinity Chapel on the north wall was built between 1430 and 1460 for the Guild of Weavers in the town. Memorial brasses to the two founder knights, Sir Richard Dixton and Sir William Prelatte, are to be found here;

both were liege men to Richard Duke of York whose portrait is in the east window. The small Garstang chapel, named after a family of northern wool merchants settled in Cirencester, is of about the same date. The present Lady Chapel was built about 1450 although evidence of the first Lady Chapel dating from c.1235 to 1250 survives in the bases of the arches leading to the Chapel. The Chapel of St Catherine dates from about 1460, and the fine wall paintings here to about the same period. St John's Chapel is late thirteenth century, the result of reconstruction then of the south side. The nave was also rebuilt, in the period 1515 to 1530.

Throughout the church are objects and furnishings of great interest. The Boleyn Cup, made for Queen Anne Boleyn in 1535, is displayed in a niche set in an arch to the right of the chancel. As beautiful in its own way is the fan-vaulted ceiling of St Catherine's Chapel, the work in 1508 of Abbot John Hakebourne. The pulpit is pre-Reformation. The font, restored now to the church after having spent over a century in the churchyard, is fourteenth century. Before returning to the street and moving on, pass down a narrow passage to the outside of the church and pause awhile in the churchyard. From this quiet place, the various styles incorporated into what Atkyns in 1712 called simply this 'Great and Beautiful Church' may be clearly seen.

From the church, leave Market Place, cross over to Castle Street and from there, turn right into Silver Street. The fine Palladian building on the corner here, what is today Lloyd's Bank, was built as a wool-merchant's house in 1720. From the end of Silver Street, turn slightly left and then right into Park Street. The Corinium Museum in Park Street houses many of the finest remains of the Roman town. There are superb mosaics laid out as they would once have been on villa floors, displays of armour, a reconstructed chambered tomb, and finds from the Saxon and medieval periods. Quiz sheets are available for children to complete as they explore.

Continue down Park Street with the high walls and hedges of the Park (which follow the line of the Roman town walls) on the left. Turn left into Cecily Hill. This road, unusually wide in comparison with many in the town, was once the main road to Bisley and Stroud. The houses here are mostly eighteenth

The lovely south porch of St. John the Baptist's at Cirencester, reckoned by some 'the most splendid of all English church porches', stands over the relative quiet of the Market Place in Cirencester in this view of c.1910.

century, with the exception of the Old Barracks, built in 1857.

The mansion in Cirencester Park was built by the first Earl Bathurst in about 1714. What design skill the Earl had is more evident in his estates and gardens which he planned together with the poet, Alexander Pope. Pope invested some of his own capital in the enterprise: the Earl promised him 'three or four million plants out of my nursery to amuse yourself with', and we later find Pope writing how he and his patron would 'draw plans for houses and gardens . . . all very fine and beautiful in our own imagination'. It is possible to walk the seven miles to Sapperton (948033) through the park, but for further points of interest in Cirencester go back down Cecily Hill, left at the foot and immediately right into Coxwell Street.

The first house on the right, Woolgatherers, was built in the seventeenth century as a wool-merchant's residence; his warehouse still stands round the corner in Thomas Street. Many of the buildings in Coxwell Street are of the same age and the line of the houses and their common style gives the street a quiet dignity. At the end of Coxwell Street, turn left down Dollar Street (turning right will bring you via Gosditch

Street, back to the parish church and the west end of Market
Place). Dollar Street is so called from the Abbey's Dole Hall,
where alms were given, doled out, to the needy. Before turning
into Spitalgate Lane, turn left into Thomas Street. The
Weavers' Hall near Dollar Street is probably the oldest
surviving secular building in Cirencester and dates from the
early fifteenth century. St John's Hospital in Spitalgate Lane is
a late twelfth-century foundation.

From Spitalgate Lane, turn right into Dugdale Road, and,
from the car park at the end, go left through the park to the
Norman gatehouse. Children might want to spend some time
in the swing park here. Keeping to that side of the lake, a path
leads to a small bridge and then back towards the town. Before
doing so, follow the signs (it's only a short way) to the exposed
Roman wall. The section shows many features typical of such
defences, but what is interesting about this site is the evidence
from several different periods. The initial earth bank, erected
c.AD 70 to AD 100 was added to in the second and third
centuries with stone walls, and with projecting bastions in the
fourth century. The reasons for the different ground plans of
the two bastions still puzzle archaeologists. From the wall,
either retrace your steps back to the footbridge and the park or
continue to the main road south of the large roundabout. The
junction here is the site of the north-east gate to Corinium,
Verulamium Gate, guarding entry from the Fosse Way. From
here, make your way down London Road to Dyer Street and
back to the Market Place. In the park, nothing now remains
above ground to indicate the presence of the Abbey; a small
plaque positioned near the path suggests the buildings were
very extensive.

Cirencester is a good centre for discovering the local area, as
befits its status of 'capital'. Following the line of either the Fosse
Way (the A433/A429 running north-east to south-west) or
Ermin Street (the A419 south-east of the town, the A417 north-
west) will quickly bring you to the surrounding countryside.
Once away from Cirencester (or as a less hurried way of
arriving), there are several river valleys whose villages offer
much to interest.

Rendcomb (019099) is a small village on the east side of the
River Churn, off the A435. St Peter's here has very fine

A mason repairs and restores the church tower in Cirencester. The drives leading west through Cirencester Park towards Pope's Seat, Ten Rides, and eventually to Sapperton, are visible over the mason's right shoulder.

medieval screenwork, comparable to that of Fairford. The two churches share common benefactors in the Tame family; in Rendcomb's case, the son Edmund rather than John. Rendcomb College has been a boys' school since 1920. North Cerney (021079) is set back from the A435 to the foot of the North Cerney Downs. Most of the houses here are seventeenth or eighteenth century. The church, All Saints, is the third to be built on this site. Interesting features include the medieval altar, only unearthed in 1912, and the drawing of the manticore, a mythical creature part-man and part-lion. Follow the winding minor road to Bagendon (012067), a quiet little place on the edge of the Merchants' Downs. The village is rather strung-out along the valley floor which often floods, a problem for the church particularly. The church has been a benefice of Jesus College, Oxford, since 1816. Before crossing the A417 and making for Daglingworth and the Duntisbournes, the wall painting of St Christopher in St Mary Magdalen's at Baunton (022048) is well worth a visit though the village itself is not. This representation of St Christopher and the infant Christ is larger than that at Hailes near Winchcombe and differs, too, in being set within a landscape.

The Church of the Holy Rood at Daglingworth (995050) contains some lovely late Anglo-Saxon carvings although the church itself has suffered the fate of many in having been over-restored in the nineteenth century. From Daglingworth, a narrow minor road follows the west bank of the River Dunt, hardly more than a stream even if it has lent its name to four villages along its length.

Both the river and the villages take their name from a Saxon landowner by name Dunt. The second part of Duntisbourne Abbots (971079) was added after 1066 to distinguish it, as a holding of the Abbey of Gloucester, from land belonging to the Abbey of Notre Dame de Lyre at nearby Duntisbourne Leer (975075).

Duntisbourne Rouse (985060) takes its name from a Breton family to whom the land belonged, the first being Sir Roger Le Rous who died in 1294. Middle Duntisbourne needs no explanation.

Each of these villages – Middle Duntisbourne is little more than one large farm – has character. Duntisbourne Abbots, which has a youth hostel, stands on a slight rise looking south-eastwards to Duntisbourne Leer. The short walk between the two is notable for having what must be one of the longest fords in Britain as the Dunt is channelled along the road. Parts of Nutbeam Farm near Duntisbourne Leer date from the mid-fifteenth century. The buildings grouped around the shallow ford here make a very attractive scene. From Middle Duntisbourne a footpath leads through fields to the Church of St Michael's at Duntisbourne Rouse. As you come through the wood to this church, the crude Anglo-Saxon masonry of the west wall is immediately apparent. The nave at least is also Saxon, parts of the chancel early Norman. It is a delightful church in a lovely setting.

Sherborne House, whose facades were completed by the local architect, Valentine Strong of Taynton, in 1651-53. The late-thirteenth-century tower of St Mary Magdalene Church is visible to the right.

Evening sun on Arlington Row, old weavers' cottages, in the village of Bibury.

'The Cotswold Rambler' gets up steam at Toddington on the Gloucester – Warwickshire Steam Railway.

The 'Blue Devil', window 15, in St Mary's Church, Fairford.

The village of Naunton in the valley of the river Windrush, west of
Stow-on-the-Wold.

Bath from the air. To the left, the graceful curve of Royal Crescent;
to the right, the Circus.

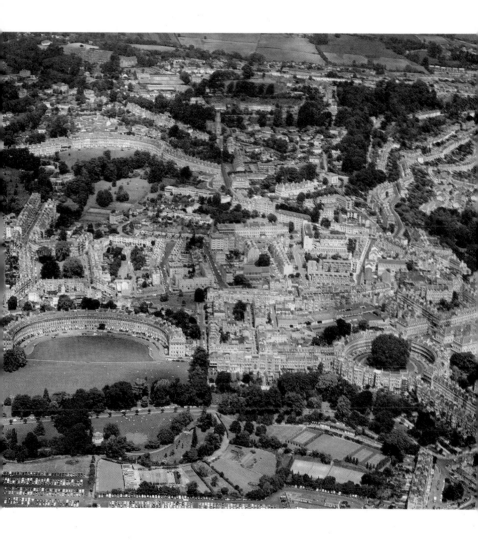

John Brown's cottage in the village of Ablington, near Bibury.
William Morris considered this the most picturesque cottage in
England.

The porch of the great Abbey Church at Malmesbury.

Like the Duntisbournes, several of the villages in the valley of the Coln share their name with the river. From Cirencester, take the A429 following the signs for Stow. At Fossebridge (081113), turn right before ascending the hill and make for Coln St Dennis (087109), a small village lying just west of the medieval Salt Way. The earliest recorded date for a village on this site is AD 804. The French connection evident in the Duntisbournes is found here too; the second part of the name reflects former ownership by the Abbey of St Denis in Paris. In the past, the church here was known as St Kenelm's after the son of Kenulf, the founder of the Abbey at Winchcombe, but it is today known as St James's.

Coln Rogers (085094) may be reached by roads on either side of the valley; the small village of Calcot is passed in taking the eastern route. Coln Rogers takes its name from one Roger of Gloucester who gave the place to the Abbey at Gloucester in the mid-twelfth century. A footpath leads from the village to the nearby hamlet of Winson (090085) which has, for such a small place, a fine classical building in Winson Manor. The attractive row of cottages north-east of the church here are mostly seventeenth century. From Winson make for Bibury (115065), crossing the river to go through the hamlet of Ablington (107077).

William Morris called Bibury 'the most beautiful village in England'. There is certainly much to interest the visitor here with the church, the museum, the trout farm, and the cottages at Arlington Row leading the list, but Morris would probably not stand by his remarks today. Bibury is really two places: Arlington to the west, and Bibury itself as the road crosses over the Coln and then swings sharply northwards to Burford. A walk from Arlington Mill Museum to Arlington Row and from there along the footpath south of the Coln to the weir on the river at Bibury Mill to return via the church and the main street is the best way to see all there is here.

The present Arlington Mill, now the Cotswold Country Museum and Gallery, dates from the seventeenth century although the Domesday survey of 1086 records a mill at Arlington. The mill was usually for corn but in the 1600s was employed as a fulling mill for the cloth produced in nearby Arlington Row. The drying cloth was hung out to dry on racks on land south of the river; the Rack Isle is today a wildfowl reserve. The Museum has interesting displays of arts and crafts furniture and of rural life including a handloom. The mill machinery, although not original to this site and now powered by motor, is eighteenth century.

Bibury Trout Farm was begun in 1902. Three million eggs are hatched annually and dispatched to stock rivers and lakes all over the world. A farm shop here sells fish and other produce. From the Trout Farm, cross the road and the Rack Isle towards Arlington Row. What is today several cottages was once a timbered-frame wool hall built to hold the wool from the Bishop of Worcester's flocks. It was converted into weavers' cottages during the seventeenth century and they are now owned by the National Trust. From the east end of the Row, a footpath leads to Bibury Mill. Bibury Court, built in 1633 and now a hotel, is situated on the opposite bank. Cross the Coln at the weir and go up the lane to the minor road. Turn left and then second left down Cemetery Lane to the parish church, St Mary's.

This attractive church has been much added to, but is in origin late Saxon. The shell of the Saxon building is marked by pilaster strips on the north and south walls of the chancel, probably indicating the original eastern extent. There is part of a Saxon cross on the exterior of the north wall. Inside, the church has some thirteenth-century stained glass and casts of Saxon grave slabs. The churchyard has a number of excellent table tombs, comparable with those at Painswick. From the church, go down Church Road to join the main street.

From Bibury, either continue down the valley of the Coln towards Coln St Aldwyns or south-east on the A433 to Barnsley (079051).

Barnsley Park is perhaps the grandest Baroque house in the Cotswolds. Built between c.1720 and 1731, the house has nine bays to its west-facing front with the central three pushed forward and framed by Corinthian pilasters. Designed most probably by John James, it is a most beautiful building inside and out and has lovely gardens. The village of Barnsley is rather spoilt in having the main road run through it, although fine seventeenth- and nineteenth-century cottages survive.

Coln St Aldwyns (144054) is bounded to the east by the

Barnsley Park showing the main facade, in a view of c.1900.

parkland of Williamstrip Park, a late seventeenth-century classical stone house. John Keble was vicar here for ten years from 1825 although the church he knew was much restored in 1853. To the east is the small village of Hatherop. The fields north-east of these two villages were the site of the now vanished Bibury Race Course which once extended across the downs between Ladbarrow Farm (172092) and Macaroni Downs Farm (185080). It was said to have been visited by Charles II and Nell Gwynne.

Quenington (144042) stands a little east of the minor road from Coln St Aldwyns, but is worth visiting for the very fine Norman doorways and tympana to the twelfth-century Church of St Swithin's. The tympanum over the north door represents the Harrowing of Hell, with Satan bound, one figure rising from the sea, another from Satan's mouth, a third from death. South from Quenington brings you to Fairford; south-west and across the droving road of the Welsh Way will take you to the Ampneys. The line of Roman Akeman Street runs west from the village, passing the curiously-named Ready Token (105046) where cash not credit was demanded of stagecoach travellers.

The Ampneys – Ampney Crucis, Ampney St Peter, and

Ampney St Mary – are attractive little villages lying close to the Ampney Brook. There are some well-preserved cottages and houses in each of the three villages, but the chief interest of each place lies in its church, especially at Ampney Crucis (065019) and the twelfth-century Church of St Mary's, now isolated from its village and south of the A417 (075015). Both have fine wall paintings, but those of St Mary's, dating from the twelfth to the fifteenth centuries, are particularly well preserved: look for the small figure of a wheelwright truing a spoke by holding it to his eye.

South of Cirencester, the Churn Valley becomes much less picturesque than to the north as the land flattens out. South Cerney (050970) is best reached from the minor road through Siddington. In the Church of All Hallows in South Cerney there is a resin copy of the surviving fragments of the South Cerney Wood Crucifix, a Romanesque crucifix figure dating to about 1130. The head, small though it is, has a wonderful grace and simplicity: it is one of the masterpieces of English Romanesque art. The niche carvings above the doorway here are very similar in style to those at Quenington and have been attributed to the same school.

The Cotswold Water Park (962054) offers a variety of entertainments although not all the lakes are open to the public. Some are still worked commercially, others are restricted to club members. On the many lakes open to the public, there are facilities for wind surfing, coarse and game fishing, and sailing one's own boat. There is a small beach for children at lake 56, south-west of Somerford Keynes (020952), but nowhere is swimming safe. The minor road from Somerford Keynes follows the River Thames whose source lies just off the A433 north of Kemble (980993). The Norman church of St Matthew's west of the small village of Coates (980010) has a particularly beautiful Early Perpendicular tower.

CHAPTER 17

Fairford, Lechlade, Cricklade and the South-East Villages

Towards the south-east of Gloucestershire and the border with Oxfordshire and Wiltshire where the rivers Coln and Leach run toward the Thames, the rolling wold landscape gives way to gentler contours, and, in places, a more open countryside. It is an area full of interest and much beauty nonetheless. Travelling south on the A361 from Burford, the main road crosses the line of Roman Akeman Street just to the north of the Cotswold Wildlife Park (245088). A little further south is the small village of Filkins (241046) set back from the main road. There is a small woollen mill here with an exhibition of past machinery as well as working looms and weaving equipment. Although the machinery is mostly more modern and the conditions certainly better, this small rurally-located industrial enterprise is probably quite typical of the ways in which cloth was produced before the advent of factory production. Guidebooks are available to tell you what each bit of machinery does. Nearby are further local craft workshops worth a visit. From Filkins, retrace your steps slightly in crossing the A361 and taking the minor road heading towards the Barringtons. Take the first turn left towards the two villages of Eastleach Martin (204052) and Eastleach Turville (198052). The Gloucestershire-Oxfordshire border is crossed at the Shire Gate.

These two charming villages lie one on either side of the River Leach. The two churches and the different names of the villages mark the former ownership of land by separate landlords. Eastleach Martin is also known as Bouthrop. The relative absence of through traffic in these villages makes for a quietness not always found in other equally attractive places, and it is well worth taking the time to stop and stroll round. Of the two churches, St Michael and St Martin is the older although it is now redundant. The original plan survives although the earliest arch was replaced in the thirteenth century during a period of rebuilding. The piers and capitals of the chancel arch are Norman. Walk from this church across the churchyard towards the gate and take the path to the left. The clapper bridge of large flagstones is known locally as 'Keble's Bridge', possibly after John Keble, a founding member of the Oxford Movement who was curate at St Michael and St Martin's from 1815 to 1825, although there have been many generations of Kebles in the manor at Eastleach Turville. Once across the river, turn right towards St Andrew's Church with its attractive saddleback tower and carved south doorway of 1130. The base of a fourteenth-century cross stands in the churchyard.

From the Eastleach's, take either of the two minor roads which lead southward towards Southrop (202035). Southrop is small even by Cotswold standards and, like too many villages in the area, its fringes have been spoilt in places by estate development. Better, though, that places are expanding and prosperous than decaying rural relics. Southrop, though small, has two claims to wider fame. It is in the eyes of most church historians the birthplace of the Oxford Movement, but its greater claim is much earlier in date: the magnificent mid-twelfth-century font in St Peter's Church. It has eight panels, three of which are of Moses with the Tablets of the Law. The other five show armoured Virtues trampling down Vices: *Modestia* (self-restraint) is to be seen beheading *Ebrietas* (drunkenness), and *Patiencia* (patience) is whipping *Ira* (anger). This font is one of the greatest glories of all the Cotswold churches.

The road from Southrop to Lechlade in places follows the route of one of the old Salt Ways, itself following an earlier route still. Lechlade stands on an ancient crossing of the Thames, and the town served as a market place for the traffic passing on what was formerly one of the main routes to Southampton and is now the A361. Building stone from Cotswold quarries was moved down the Thames from Lechlade to build St Paul's and the town was an important point of enshipment for Welsh cattle for the London markets driven down established droving roads such as the 'Welsh Way' (118027).

In 1501, the manor and town of Lechlade was part of the dower of Catherine of Aragon and the manor may also have

Thomas Pitts, an old Morris dancer from the village of Eastleach Martin, from a photograph taken about 1885.

been part of the dower of Katherine Parr. The church, along with Fairford, Cirencester, and Northleach, is one of the finest wool churches of the Cotswolds. It is dedicated to St Lawrence, a popular Spanish saint, a dedication it owes to the town's connections with Catherine of Aragon. St Lawrence was martyred by being cooked on a griddle. There is a small image of the saint holding a gridiron in a chancel window.

Lechlade's former principal function is evident in the large market place which, though it is now rather spoilt by being used for car parking, is surrounded by some fine buildings. Most are early eighteenth century, but perhaps the finest piece of architecture is St John's Bridge over the Thames, built by one Peter Fitzherbert about 1229 though altered in places in the nineteenth century.

From Lechlade, it is possible to visit the remaining places mentioned in this chapter in the order they follow below, or, in reverse order, by beginning at Fairford (155010). Either way, leave Lechlade on the A417 travelling towards Fairford. Various sailing and water-skiing facilities are available at the sailing club to the south of this road about two miles from Lechlade. Kempsford (161968) once had a castle but depends for its defence today on RAF Fairford immediately to the north. The outstanding church of St Mary's here has a very fine Norman nave and is sited a little to the north-east of where the castle once stood. John of Gaunt was responsible for the tower, built between 1385 and 1399, and raised as a tribute to his first wife, Lady Blanche of Lancaster, patron of Chaucer, who is said to have written a poem in honour of her marriage in Kempsford. From Kempsford, follow the signs to Castle Eaton (146958), and from there, the minor road south-westwards to join the A419 just past Seven Bridges (124926). The main road here follows the line of the Ermin Way, the Roman road running south-east out of Cirencester. Turn towards Cirencester and almost immediately leave the main road on the B4040 to Cricklade.

Cricklade (100932), like Lechlade, is an Anglo-Saxon town and, like Lechlade, occupies an important position on the Thames. The remains of the town's Saxon walls may just be discerned to the east of the B4041. Cricklade lies on the very fringes of our region, and although the town has made quite extensive use of Cotswold stone, it lacks something of the character of places more properly Cotswold. Most of the old part of the town is along both sides of the High Street running almost north-south. The church is dedicated to St Sampson, a Celtic saint, and most of the present building dates from the second half of the thirteenth century. St Mary's Church to the north end of the High Street is older, having been built in the early 1100s. As you make your way down the High Street towards St Mary's, look out for the large Jubilee Clock erected to commemorate Queen Victoria's silver jubilee in 1897. The Vale Hotel stands on the corner at the junction of the High Street with the Bath Road which, as the name suggests, was once one of the main roads in the area to Bath. Like many towns in the south Cotswolds, Cricklade had interests in the manufacture of textiles. Today only Ockwells, the glove makers located to the east side at the southern end of the High Street,

On the magnificent mid-twelfth-century font at Southrop, the names of the Virtues are inscribed on the arches of the panels, those of the Vices backwards on the panels themselves. In this picture, restraint triumphs by beheading drunkenness.

continues as a commercial operation a trade first mentioned in the town in 1590. A small museum located in Calcutt Street and run by the Cricklade Historical Society (who have also produced a town trail pamphlet) has displays and information about Cricklade in the past but opening times are limited.

To the north of the town is the 110-acre North Meadow, a site of great botanical interest designated a National Nature Reserve in 1973. It is an ancient flood meadow, and the traditional holding and working of the meadow as Lammas Land with stock grazed from August 12th to February 12th and hay taken in the summer has, together with the exclusion of all artificial fertilisers, resulted in a wide variety of rare plants. Rather than leave the town to the north by following the line of the old Roman causeway, now the B4041, retrace your earlier route on the B4040, and for a short way take the A419 towards Cirencester. Turn right in the direction of Marston Meysey (129972). Passing through the village, head towards Meysey Hampton (119999), rather than taking the first turning to Fairford. Meysey Hampton is well worth this brief detour. Follow the signpost to the little church of St Mary the Virgin which, standing on a small knoll which affords good views to the north, is a delight. It lay at its foundation within the Diocese of the Bishop of Worcester and was consecrated by him in 1269. Apart from the very fine Early English style of the great part of the church itself, look out for the early alms box near the church door, the carved lectern dated 1622 and the memorial erected in 1630 to James Vaulx, a local physician. From Meysey Hampton, turn eastwards on the A417 to Fairford.

Fairford is sited on the banks of the River Coln, a popular river with fishermen. The river has been canalised as it runs through Fairford Park and the best view of the town and certainly of St Mary's, Fairford's magnificent church, is from the west with the river in the foreground and the church to the top of the slight rise behind. The London Road running through the centre of the town has several late seventeenth- and eighteenth-century buildings along its length such as Morgan Hall and, set slightly back from the road to the east, Eastend House. But the real glory of Fairford and the thing that attracts visitors more than any other is the church, and, in the church, the stained glass. It really can't be rushed: if you've come straight from Lechlade and want to visit those other places mentioned above but time is short, stay in Fairford and leave the others for a later day. If you've already done them, then be prepared to be late for supper because Fairford's windows are truly awe-inspiring.

Leaving aside the base of the tower, St Mary's Church was almost entirely rebuilt in the last decade of the fifteenth century by John Tame and later by his son, Edmund. Tame was a wool stapler and cloth merchant from Cirencester and, like many of his type and in an age of different values, sought

The Market Place, Fairford, in a postcard view of c.1910.

to use his worldly wealth to erect a lasting sacred memorial. In twenty-eight windows the stained glass covers an area of over 2000 square feet. Apart from being removed for safety during the Second World War, it has never been removed other than to a limited extent for restoration, and with the exception of parts of three west windows which were damaged in a storm in 1703, the windows represent a complete set of medieval stained glass.

On entering the church, make your way across the nave and stand with your back to the organ: opposite you is the first window. Most of the windows have four panels. In the first panel of window 1, Eve is shown disobeying God by taking fruit from the tree of knowledge, the fruit being offered by a blue-headed serpent. The remainder of this first window shows Moses and the burning bush, Gideon and the Fleece, and the Queen of Sheba offering a silver casket to Solomon. The windows are numbered from here and it is quite easy to follow the biblical narrative as it unfolds. Windows 2, 3 and 4 in the Lady Chapel employ glorious colour in their depictions of the marriage of Joseph and Mary, for example, and the scene of Christ and the Doctors in the Temple depicts the Christ Child with an old head on young shoulders, as his audience is clearly finding in listening to him. Before passing on to the next window, pause in the Lady Chapel at the Lygon Tomb (c.1560) and the brasses to Sir Edmund Tame, son of the founder. The bones of John Tame lie under a large polished slab of Purbeck Marble with memorial brasses to himself and Alice his wife. Window 6 shows the Descent from the Cross and the Entombment. The last of the three panels in this window has a wonderful cameo of an impenitent spirit trapped behind red hot bars within the larger picture. Further windows as you move round the church show the Apostles (windows 10, 11 and 12), and other teachers of the faith (window 13). Windows 17 to 20 show evangelists and prophets and 21 to 24 twelve martyrs and confessors of the faith including, in window 23, Charlemagne and St Edward the Confessor. Before moving to these, spend some time at Window 15. The whole suite of windows is, of course, a moralising and instructional guide for those in the past without access to a printed copy of the Scriptures. But this window in particular seems to convey more vividly than most the horrors of damnation and the torment to be suffered by those who stray from the paths of righteousness. Above the transom Christ sits with the world as his footstool; kneeling are John the Baptist and Christ's holy mother. Beneath the transom and immediately beneath Christ in the central section of the window stands St Michael, resplendent in a suit of golden armour. He is holding a balance; in the left a devil is attempting to tip the scales but the weight of the saved soul to the right is too great. In two right-hand panels, fallen souls are being hounded into hell by hordes of devils, one of whom, in blue with a beard, is taking an old man off to his doom in a wheelbarrow. In the bottom two lights sits Satan himself with his sharp teeth and staring eyes – a final warning to the impenitent. There are other terrifying representations of devils in the small window lights of windows 25 to 28 which show persecutors of the Church.

As beautiful as the windows and with the same didactic intent are the wood carvings of the misericords in the chancel. There are different scenes including a grotesque head, a fox with geese, a dog sniffing for meat whilst his mistress spins, a wheatsheaf and reapers, and a lovely carving of the battle between the sexes (with Woman winning) as a wife belabours her husband.

CHAPTER 18

Tetbury and Malmesbury

The countryside along the Gloucestershire-Wiltshire border south-west of Cirencester, although more open and with wider and more distant views than the rolling hills further north, is no less Cotswold in character. In some of the villages, it is true, the buildings have a different style, but in the two principal towns of the area, Tetbury and Malmesbury, the use of local stone in traditional ways has produced some of the loveliest architecture of the whole region.

Tetbury (892935) may be reached from Cirencester via the A433, the Fosse Way, the modern road leaving the Roman route (which goes on to form the county boundary) about halfway between the two towns. For a less direct and quieter route, leave the A433 past the Thames Head Inn, near the source of the River Thames, and turn right towards Tarlton (960994), a small village whose church has a good Norman chancel arch and interesting roof arches. From there, minor roads, gated in places, lead through Lowesmoor Farm to Cherington (902986), or south-west to Rodmarton (942980).

Cherington is an attractive village with several fine eighteenth-century cottages, some in short terraces not always typical of the area. Rodmarton, many of whose buildings were restored in the nineteenth century, centres around a triangular village green with the church, St Peter's, to the northern side. Near the church, which has some fine 'tea-caddy' graves and an interesting mid-fifteenth-century memorial brass in the chancel, is the old School House, dated 1828. The village is of particular interest for its Manor, which although 'modern' in being built between 1909 and 1926, is largely in 'traditional' Cotswolds style in its mullioned windows and string courses if not in its ground plan. It is the finest single representation of the work of Ernest Barnsley. The Manor, privately owned, can be seen from the road south of the village.

Tetbury is a lovely town with a pleasant and welcoming 'feel' to it as well as some splendid buildings. There are car parks at the Chipping, the site of the original market place and further out on the B4067 near the cattle market (to the foot of Gumstool Hill). The best place to start a walk around the town is in Market Place and at the Town Hall or Market House. Tetbury has been a market town since at least the end of the twelfth century. There is still a weekly market, but the trade in modern consumer goods and foodstuffs in no way matches the former trade in cloth and wool. The present Town Hall or Market House, a wonderful example of the type, was built in 1655 and altered in part in 1817. The visitor has a choice of several walks round the town from this central point.

Church Street is mainly seventeenth century, but some of the buildings have been rather spoiled by modern shop frontages. Nothing remains of the medieval church nor of 'Tetta's monastery' mentioned in a Saxon charter of 681. The present church, St Mary's, was built in 1781 and until 1890 incorporated the spire of the medieval building. The present spire, as elegant in its way as the church itself, is a landmark for miles around. From the church, either continue downhill toward the Bath Bridge (A433), built c.1775 (there is a wonderful view of the church from this point), or make your way through the churchyard to the lane to the north and then turn right towards Silver Street and the Green. Most of the town houses here date from the seventeenth century: look for one with a magnificent 'shell shape' to its portico.

Chipping Street connects the present Market Place with the Chipping. On the west side of the Chipping are several Georgian houses; to the east, some buildings have medieval remains, incorporated behind later frontages. Look for the passage between Nos. 5 and 13, thought to be a screens passage from a medieval hall. The Chipping Steps lead from the north-east corner of the square towards the attractive buildings of Chipping Croft and Croft Cottage set back from the B4067. Turning right and right again here brings you back to the Market Place via Gumstool Hill.

Long Street, curving north-westwards away from the Market Place, has a number of fine stone houses. Several, like the Close Hotel and, further down, the Porch House, date from the 1600s. Most of the others are eighteenth century although they stand on much earlier sites. The Tourist Information Office on

Crowds gather for the Tetbury Carnival procession, c.1910.

the corner with the Cirencester Road (A433) has a small Tetbury Police Bye-Gones Museum in the Old Courthouse.

North-west of Tetbury, on a minor road off the A434 to Avening, is the lovely Elizabethan manor of Chavenage House (872951). The 'E-shaped' buildings laid out by Edward Stephens in 1576 have been distorted in plan by later additions to the rear, but alterations on the whole have been remarkably sensitive. South-west of Chavenage, on the A4135 from Tetbury, is the village of Beverston (862939). The castle, built c.1200 by Maurice de Gaunt, underwent extensive rebuilding in the mid-fourteenth century and again in the early seventeenth century; the medieval castle is represented in the impressive Great or Berkeley Tower and the gatehouse. The castle chapel which occupies the whole of the first floor is one of the finest examples in the country.

South of Tetbury, the A434 leads directly to Malmesbury. For a less direct but quieter route, take the A433 out of Tetbury and turn left through Shipton Moyne (891895) where the village pub has the charming name of The Cat and Custard Pot! An even less direct way still of arriving at Malmesbury is to follow the A433 south-west of Tetbury as far as Didmarton, take minor roads south to join the B4040 at Sherston, and then make for Malmesbury along the attractive valley of the Avon.

Highgrove House, north of Doughton (878913) and hidden from view from the A433, is the country residence of the Prince and Princess of Wales. Further along this road is the Westonbirt Arboretum (847899), begun in 1829 by Robert Stayner Holford and since 1956 maintained by the Forestry Commission. The Arboretum is at its most colourful in autumn as many of the trees turn golden-russet shades, but the spring is lovely, too, for the flowering shrubs. But even the shape of the trees, individually and in groups and avenues, is lovely. The Visitor Centre has guidebooks to the several trails through the Arboretum.

Didmarton (820874) has many good eighteenth- and nineteenth-century houses along the length of the main road, but the chief delight here has to be St Lawrence's Church, situated on a slight rise at the east end of the village south of the A433. This church is interesting because it escaped Victorian restoration; what survives today is a remarkable example of a medieval church in eighteenth-century condition. There are fine large box pews and a 'three-decker' pulpit positioned at the junction of the L-shaped church in order to see in both directions. Now unfortunately redundant, it is a charming building.

From Didmarton, take the road south through the hamlet of Sopworth (828862) and turn eastwards at the crossroad near Hundred Acre Farm towards Sherston (854860). Sherston will be known by some for its wine company, whose offices are opposite the parish church. Sherston village is first recorded in AD 896 as 'Scorranstan' from the Old English 'sceard-stan', meaning a boundary stone. This in turn became 'Sorstain' and 'Sorestone' before the present name was regularly used from about 1280. From Sherston, it is possible to take the B4040 to Malmesbury through the village of Easton Grey (882876) or to reach it via the minor roads south of the River Avon and the village of Foxley. The buildings around the weirs at Easton Grey present a most charming scene, and a little further south, a track along the river's southern bank crosses a footbridge on the line of the Roman Fosse Way, with the Roman settlement, White Walls, on the northern bank (884873). No trace of this fifty-acre site now remains visible.

How quiet without the motor car: the mid-seventeenth-century Market House, standing on its squat Tuscan pillars, presides over almost empty streets in this 1900 view of central Tetbury.

Malmesbury (935872) lays claim to being the oldest borough in England. It is the birthplace of William of Malmesbury, the great historian, born c.1095, and of Thomas Hobbes, the philosopher, born in 1588. Other worthy citizens who have brought fame to this lovely town include Athelstan, one of the greatest of Saxon kings; Elmer (or Oliver), the flying monk, who, in about 1005, flew from the west tower of the Abbey and survived (despite breaking both legs); and Adhelm, Abbot from c.675, who succeeded the Celtic monk, Mailduib, from whom the town takes its name. There are some fine buildings in the town, and in the carvings of the south porch to the abbey church, Malmesbury has one of the most glorious architectural treasures in the whole country.

The present abbey church remains represent about a third of the twelfth-century buildings. An earlier wooden abbey, together with much of the town, was destroyed by fire in about 1050, having itself replaced a building burned by Danish raiders in 850. Following the Dissolution of the Abbey in December 1539, only nine bays in the nave of the original building remained and this total was reduced to six after the collapse of the west tower in 1662. Despite this continued reduction in extent, there is still much to see.

The nave, today much as it has been since alterations in the late fourteenth century, has a freshness of tone resulting from the use throughout of light-coloured box stone from quarries in the south Cotswolds, and a grandeur produced by the massive late Romanesque pillars. Look up on the south wall of the nave for the 'watching-loft', which may have been used to view services taking place behind the rood screen or as a place of penance. The roof of the nave has been restored in the twentieth century. A large mirror, placed like a table in the centre of the nave, shows this wonderful roof to great advantage. In the north aisle is the medieval commemorative tomb to King Athelstan, who died in 939. Athelstan's actual place of burial is not known now, since his remains were moved and reburied repeatedly in later centuries. In the west end of the south aisle, modern stained-glass windows commemorate Mailduib and the other notables mentioned above. Elmer, the flying monk, may be seen holding a set of wings; both he and they are in one piece.

The south porch, now the main entrance to the abbey church, is magnificent and awe-inspiring. It is a visual aid to worship. The inner arch shows the story of the Creation. The middle arch has scenes from the Old Testament, and the outer arch depicts events in the life of Christ. The sides of the porch are also heavily carved and show the twelve apostles. Above the inner door is a tympanum of Christ in Majesty flanked by angels. The suggestion has been made that the carvings in the porch (and other architectural features) reflect the influence of craftsmen from Burgundy and south-west France, there having been a Burgundian abbot, Peter Moraunt, settled here in 1141. It is now thought more likely, however, that Malmesbury Abbey shared with places like Old Sarum and churches in the south-west Cotswolds the skills of a distinct local school of masons which flowered especially between the 1170s and the early thirteenth century.

From the porch, take the path across the churchyard and

through the eighteenth-century Tolsey Gate into the Market Square. The Market Cross here, built about 1490 'for poore market folkes to stand dry when rayne commith', was restored in 1980. From here, go down the High Street with its principally eighteenth-century buildings and enter Cross Hayes. The Tourist Information Office and the Athelstan Museum are housed in the Town Hall, on the north side of the square. Go across Cross Hayes and down Silver Street and Back Hill steps towards the river.

Back Hill steps mark the edge of the old town and, in particular, the site of the Little or Merle Gate. At their foot, turn right along St John's Street. The Courthouse of Malmesbury's Old Corporation is set back to the left. The Old Corporation are the descendants of those men to whom Athelstan granted common land. The land is still held and passed down to new generations as common land. The late seventeenth-century almshouses of St John near here have a thirteenth-century arch set in the wall facing the Lower High Street.

Go along the Lower High Street and past the Roundhouse, which may once have been a gatehouse, and follow the path along the King's Wall. Bear right after a short way through what was Postern Gate and into Bird Cage Walk beside the remains of the thirteenth-century church of St Paul's Without (without the Abbey grounds). From here, it is a short way along Gloucester Street back to the Abbey.

CHAPTER 19

Wotton-under-Edge and the South-West Wold-Edge Villages

The roughly triangular area of the Cotswolds between North Nibley to the north-west, Horton to the south and the junction of the A46(T) with the A4135 east of the tiny hamlet of Newington Bagpath has some of the finest views in the whole of the Cotswolds. Several small villages situated on the scarp edge stand also at the entrance to small yet deep and secluded valleys, or Cotswold 'bottoms' as they are known locally: North Nibley to Waterley Bottom, the village of Coombe north of Wotton-under-Edge to Tyley Bottom, and the small villages of Wortley and Alderley to Ozleworth Bottom. Driving, or more especially, walking along these quiet valleys with their lower slopes in pasture and their tops in woodland is to discover a genuinely unspoilt countryside. The largest of these valley and scarp-edge settlements is the small town of Wotton-under-Edge, its name the best clue to its situation.

Wotton-under-Edge (757933) is really three towns in one: the first is evident in the unplanned streets and lanes around the parish church, St Mary's the Virgin: the second in the 'Old Town' and the streets between and including Long Street and Symn Lane; and the third, the more recent (though no better planned) modern town which sprawls across the adjacent hillsides. Perhaps the best place to start the discovery of the old and the new Wotton is at the church (there's a small car park off Potters Pond and a larger one in The Chipping, off Market Street). The present church dates from 1283 but stands on the site of an older building. It is broad and airy inside. The most interesting features are the organ, a gift from George I in 1726 to St Martin-in-the-Fields and brought here in 1799, and the late fourteenth-century brasses, amongst the finest in the Cotswolds. From the churchyard, take the footpath down the lane to Potters Pond and turn right towards the white-painted Ram Inn. This is the oldest building in Wotton, its fourteenth-century timbering standing in contrast to many of the town's later stone-built buildings. Go up the hill towards the town

172

centre – look for the mill buildings of Waterloo Mill (now a private residence) to the rear of the car park – and go past the site of the old Grammar School, founded in 1384, on the corner of School Road. From the war memorial, turn down Church Street and into Long Street, one of the main shopping streets in the town. Number 13 Long Street has an original Tudor studded door, but otherwise many of the best features of the buildings here are obscured at ground level by shop fronts. The rectangle of streets of which Long Street is one side is the 'second Wotton', the town planned as a new borough by the Berkeleys in 1252. Market Street has several fine houses of the medieval period, most having only been saved from collapse by restoration in the mid-1970s. A right turn at Bear Street at the top of the High Street will bring you to the top of the Old Town. As you go downhill toward the church, look for the Old Town Mill on the left. This building, dated 1817, is typical of the smaller steam-powered mills once common in the region. Wotton never had the larger mills and factories found to the north in places like Nailsworth and Chalford.

Just out of Wotton on the B4058 towards Nailsworth and on a sharp right-hand bend in the road near the village of Coombe, is a remarkable 'flight' of strip lynchets. These are ancient fields, the result of continued ploughing along the side of hills such that the ploughshare turned the soil downhill, and, eventually, formed sequences of flatter slopes and terraces. A local tradition has it that the lynchets near Coombe and elsewhere on the escarpment around Wotton were used by the Cistercian monks of Kingswood Abbey for their vineyards. There are further flights of lynchets of the slopes of Wotton Hill, off the B4060 towards North Nibley and Dursley.

The road from Wotton to North Nibley (741958) passes several good examples of larger seventeenth-century farm buildings in places like Bournstream and Southend, and to the west on leaving Wotton, there are wonderful views out across the vales towards the Severn and the Forest of Dean. North Nibley is overlooked by the Tyndale Monument, built in 1866 as a memorial to William Tyndale, born here in 1484 and the first to translate the Bible into English.

A footpath leads to the monument: it's worth the steep climb for the views at the top. From North Nibley, minor roads lead uphill through the tiny hamlets of Forthay and Millend and join the main road into Dursley. These roads are little more than lanes and are very steep in places. Walking is much the best way to discover the quiet charms of Waterley Bottom and other secluded valleys here.

South-west from Wotton-under-Edge, the B4058 leads away from the Cotswolds and towards the villages of the vales. Places like Charfield (722922) and Kingswood (745918) reflect in the use of brick and limestone their position on the borders of these two distinct regions. The gatehouse is the only surviving feature of Kingswood Abbey, founded in 1139 though not really properly established until 1147. Wickwar (723887) is the largest of the nearby vale villages and, from here, a minor road leads across the open ground of Inglestone Common and Hawkesbury Common back towards the Cotswolds' edge.

Wortley (765916) and Alderley (769909) are both tiny places situated where the attractive slopes of Ozleworth Bottom meet the escarpment. A minor road along the northern flanks of this lovely valley turns sharply uphill at the head of the valley towards the hamlet of Ozleworth (792933). The small church of St Nicholas here is worth stopping at. Go through the gates at the corner of the road and down the lane past the well-situated eighteenth-century house of Ozleworth Park. The church stands in a circular walled churchyard unusual for the Cotswolds. It is possible that it stands on the site of a much older, perhaps pre-Christian place of worship. The church, now redundant, is of interest for its slightly lop-sided hexagonal tower (the longest side is to the east). This is a very rare feature and only a few such towers survive elsewhere in Britain. Much of the interior was rather cruelly treated in the restoration of 1873.

From Ozleworth, carry on up the hill until the road levels out. A right turn at the top, past the radio transmitter, will bring you to the small village of Newington Bagpath (818948), today little more than a farm. But the place was once larger and more important as the decayed church and the motte and bailey remains of a castle owned by the Berkeleys would suggest. There are several lovely walks here, past the castle mound and on down the rounded valley slopes towards Lasborough with its attractively-situated church and from there

The rare central hexagonal tower at St. Nicholas's church, Ozleworth, probably dates from the time of the church's founder, Roger Berkeley, who died in 1131.

to Boxwell, or west across the fields to Bagpath. Boxwell and Boxwell Court, a good survival from the late 1400s, can also be reached from the A46(T).

Newark Park, reached on minor roads west of Ozleworth, is one of the finest larger country houses in the Cotswolds. Approached across parkland, the house is superbly situated on the edge of the hill with wonderful views down the valley. The present house is largely the work of James Wyatt in about 1790, but remains of a much earlier house, dating from 1550 and said to have been built after the Dissolution from the stones of Kingswood Abbey, survive in the east front. Newark Park is one of a pair of houses built of Kingswood stone by Nicholas Poyntz, former steward to the abbey. The other, and Poyntz's principal residence, is Acton Court, north of Iron Acton in the vale (678842). Newark Park is open to the public though the times are limited.

The first village on the scarp edge south of Alderley is Hillesley (769897), an attractive if small place. Like Alderley and many other such villages, Hillesley was once involved in a small way in cloth manufacture. Agriculture is the principal source of employment today. Midger Wood, at the head of the Kilcott Valley, is a small nature reserve with lovely 'hangars' of beech trees on the escarpment. From the wood, a footpath runs across the open downland to the tiny hamlet of Tresham and from there to Ozleworth Bottom. From Hillesley, two minor roads lead south. It is possible to get spectacular views out over the vales and beyond from both, but motorists will find the 'top' road the easier. The oriental-looking monument that stands near the junction with a minor road leading down from the scarp edge (and which eventually leads to Wickwar) is the Somerset tower, built in 1846 as a memorial to General Somerset. Continue south towards the village of Hawkesbury Upton (780870). Just before this village, turn off the road at a triangular-shaped pond and go downhill towards Hawkesbury (768869). The tower of St Mary's is the first sign that you are coming to a village. With its neat square-trimmed yew trees in the churchyard and impressive tower, the church is something of a misfit, if an attractive one, in a place of this size. As you stand at the entrance gate to the churchyard, look across at the small flight of strip lynchets on the western side of Hawkesbury Knoll.

Horton (766850) is principally of interest for Horton Court. Part of the north wing of this house was built in 1140 and the Court can with some justification claim to be one of the oldest inhabited houses in the Cotswolds. The rest of the house, which is a National Trust property and is open to the public for part of the year, dates from about 1521 and was built for William Knight. Knight spent some time in Rome as envoy of Henry VIII, and both house and garden contain elements of design in the Italian style. From Horton, minor roads either continue south to Little Sodbury or east to join with the main A46(T) as it bisects the south Cotswolds.

CHAPTER 20

Badminton, Dyrham, and the South Cotswolds

Discovering the south Cotswolds is to discover, in miniature, the Cotswolds as a whole. There are secluded valleys on the scarp edge, wide and lovely views, villages high on the open wolds, manor houses and large managed estates. One of the largest estates and houses in the area is Badminton, north of the village of Great Badminton (808828). Badminton is best known for its sporting connections: its horse trials, an international three-day event held, usually, early in May, and the racquet game that bears its name. The first continues in a modern form the long-standing involvement of Badminton and the Dukes of Beaufort with the horse and sport. The 5th Duke is credited with having introduced foxhunting to the Cotswolds in the 1760s. His heir, the 8th Duke, entertained over 2000 horsemen on one occasion in the 1860s. Today, daily crowds of 200,000 people for the international three-day eventing are not uncommon. The second sport, badminton itself, was first played in the entrance hall on the north front of the house: the modern court still uses these dimensions.

Like many such houses and their gardens, Badminton House and Park incorporates the work of several periods and builders. And what is there now is as much the result of the clearing away of the old as it is the creation of an entirely new landscape: the present church of St Michael's, for example, which is attached to the house, was built only in 1785, the earlier medieval church which lay further to the west being then demolished. In the extensive grounds, few of the radiating avenues planned in the late seventeenth century now survive. They were cleared in about 1746 by the landscape gardener William Kent as part of his contract to improve the 'prospect' of the estate. His designs were, in turn, modified by 'Capability' Brown, but the greater part of Badminton Park today is Kent's work. And very fine it is, too. In Worcester Lodge (811872), to the north of the estate on the A433 west of Didmarton, Kent created perhaps the finest example of a

Badminton village, looking west, in 1900.

Palladian summer house in Britain. Elsewhere in the grounds are a number of interesting park buildings. The aptly-named Ragged Castle, built about 1750 near the north drive to the house, is a folly. Others, like the castellated Castle Barn and other ornate farm buildings, combine style with more workaday functions.

The seventeenth-century architect of the house is unknown. Later additions to the principal north-facing block were made by 1740, and the two attached pavilions are probably the work of Kent about 1748. The interior has been remodelled on several occasions, but always sensitively so. The house, which is not open to the public, stands north of the village of Great Badminton. Like many estate villages, Great Badminton has a not unpleasing uniformity of style and standard in its buildings, the grand almshouses of 1714 on the south side of the main street being especially noteworthy, even if the pale peach limewash is not to everyone's taste.

From Great Badminton, take the road signposted Acton Turville (809809). This is the largest, though not the most charming, of a cluster of small villages on the south-eastern borders of the Cotswolds. From Acton Turville, take the B4039 south and a little way after crossing the M4, turn south again at the village of Burton towards Nettleton and West Kington. West Kington (812774) was once the charge of Hugh Latimer, one-time bishop of Worcester, who was burnt at the stake (or martyred depending on your viewpoint), with Ridley in Oxford on 16th October 1555. From here, take the minor roads that cross the Fosse Way and make for the village of Castle Combe. Together with the villages of Stanton in the central Cotswolds and Great Tew in the Oxfordshire wolds, Castle Combe (842771) must be one of the most attractive and unspoilt villages in England. Although it is known that both Romans and Saxons had fortifications here, the village takes its name from the castle built here in 1135 by the de Dunstanvilles. All that remains today of the castle is an impressively-sited motte and bailey north of the village. The village centres around the covered Market Cross. This is as good a place as any from which to start a walk around (cars may be parked south of the village or in the large car park up the hill past the Museum). The Market Cross stands next to the smaller Butter Cross, which is thought to stand where a second market cross stood before its destruction in 1840. From here, a short path leads to St Andrew's Church. Apart from the tower which is original and was built in 1436, the church was almost entirely rebuilt in the middle years of the nineteenth century in the exact style of the then existing church, said to be in danger of collapse. Restored as it is, the church is less interesting than the village houses, but there is a very rare and faceless medieval clock here, still working, and a fine font with a bookrest attachment to the bowl. On the outside, look for the small carving high in the right-hand corner on the east side of the tower. This is a carving of a weaver's shuttle and shears, a testimony to the basis of Castle Combe's prosperity in the past. 'Castle Combe' was a red or white cloth of high quality.

From the church, go down the main street toward the bridge over the By Brook. The village was maintained as part of a manorial estate until 1947 and it is pleasing to see that later owner occupancy, from natives and incomers alike, has not been allowed to spoil the scene. Look for the street lamps and television aerials (there are none and what a difference it makes). Most of the houses date from the mid-sixteenth century or earlier, though most have been much altered within. The weavers' cottages in Water Lane and the larger Weavers' House here, formerly two houses, are the only remaining

Crowds watch as horse and rider skilfully negotiate one of the many fences during the three-day eventing at Badminton Horse Trials.

buildings known to have been connected with the cloth trade. From the end of Water Lane and left of the Pack Bridge, a footpath marks the start of the Rack Hill Nature Trail. (An explanatory leaflet and map are available in the Post Office.) As with Rack Isle in Bibury, this hill takes its name from having been the place where cloths were racked on tenterhooks to dry.

Returning along the same route, go back up the village street towards the Market Cross. Archway Cottage to the left is all that remains of two buildings once the gatehouses to the manor, now a hotel and reached via West Street. Continue up the hill towards Upper Manor House, notable for its shell portico. However attractive this is to some, the later addition of this ornamentation also rather detracts from the original fifteenth-century building. Further up the hill still, the local museum has exhibits and displays relating to the village. For motorcycle enthusiasts, the Castle Combe racing circuit is best reached from the B4039.

From Castle Combe, minor roads lead to Slaughterford (840740), so called because of the defeat here of invading Danes by 'native' Saxons, and to North Wraxall (819751) where more recent battles are fought over house prices as developers keen to turn old farm buildings into houses the villagers cannot afford too rapidly alter the character of the village. Colerne (820710) stands on the hilltops overlooking the By Brook and the Box Valley. The village of Box (826685) and the nearby quarries provided much of the building freestone used in the southern Cotswolds before quarrying ceased in 1936.

Up the hill east of the village on the A4(T) to Corsham is the west entrance to the famous Box Tunnel. Built under the direction of Isambard Kingdom Brunel between 1836 and 1841, the tunnel runs dead straight for 3,212 yards. So true a piece of engineering is it that on one day in the year (around April 8th), the rising sun in the east may be seen through the west end of the tunnel.

The Fosse Way comes down over the scarp slopes west of Box and into the Avon Valley at Batheaston. The Three Shire Stones (796700), marking the former meeting-point of Gloucestershire, Wiltshire and Somerset, are not what they appear: this is a fake nineteenth-century megalith. From the valley, steep minor roads climb the scarp towards the villages of Cold Ashton and Marshfield. Unlike its neighbour which in its exposed position is aptly named, the name Marshfield (780738) is misleading. The village takes its name from being near the 'marches' or borders between counties rather than from anything to do with boggy country. The village is really one long street, the result of development along a former main coaching route. Marshfield was established as a market town as early as 1266, but most of the many good buildings here, even in the older east end, date from no earlier than the late seventeenth century. Cold Ashton (749726) is set back from the main A420. The village is unexceptional although the manor house is an attractive building in a good setting. From the village, take the A46 south for only a little way before turning off right and downhill. These minor roads are an attractive, if slower way, of getting to Bath. As the lane descends the side of the valley through a scatter of pleasing cottages, turn right up the lane signposted Langridge. Langridge (740695) is just that, a tiny place on the long eastern edge of Lansdown Hill. This hill is the site of Bath racecourse, but it has seen more dramatic action in the Civil War battle here in 1643. The battle here was

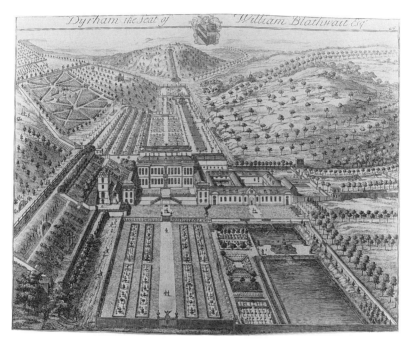

Kip's 1709 engraving of Dyrham Park may 'over-formalise' the layout of the gardens but gives a good idea of their extent and grandeur (from Atkyn's *The Ancient and Present State of Glocestershire,* second edition 1768).

a Pyrrhic victory for the Royalists, who lost not only about half their cavalry but also their commanding officer, Sir Bevil Grenville. A monument at the north end of the hill commemorates both Grenville and the battle. The Cotswold Way runs along the scarp edge here and there are wonderful views both north and south. As the Way crosses a stone stile near the edge, look across at the bumps in the flat field. These mark the house plots and walls of a deserted medieval settlement: on a cold day with a sharp wind, it is not hard to understand why it was deserted.

Leaving Lansdown Hill to the north, make for Dyrham either by going past Tracy Park (now a golf and country club) and through the village of Doynton, or by skirting the eastern slopes of Freezing Hill to join the A46(T). If going by the latter, take the time to look at the 'flights' of strip lynchets on both sides of the valley.

Dyrham (738757) is best known for Dyrham Park, the home of the Blathwayts since the end of the seventeenth century. In contrast to Badminton, almost everything is known about the builders and architects of Dyrham Park. The principal architect from 1692 was Samuel Hauduroy, a French designer and painter as well as architect. Later additions were made by several local masons and by William Talman, Christopher Wren's deputy-in-command in London. Seen from the west across the lawns with the twelfth-century St Peter's Church partly visible on the wooded slope to the left, Dyrham Park is a quite outstanding example of an eighteenth-century country residence. The gardens, too, are a delight, laid out in the Dutch manner with the attention to detail regarding water typical of that style. Dyrham Park has been a National Trust property since 1957.

Dodington Park (752798) is another fine south Cotswolds country house and garden. An earlier house of c.1650 at Dodington Park was almost entirely rebuilt by James Wyatt, who was also responsible for Newark Park and Lasborough Park further north. In contrast to the usual way in which such houses and grounds were laid out, the house here is later than the gardens, designed in 1764 by Capability Brown with his characteristic feel for the natural 'lie of the land', by some thirty years. East of Dodington Park, the small village of Tormarton (768789) derives its name in much the same way as Marshfield to the south: from the tower ('tor') of the church and 'mearc' from the Old English for marches or boundary. The village stood on the boundary between the Saxon kingdoms of Mercia and Wessex and is now quiet and unassuming.

North of Tormarton and Dodington, the villages of Old and Little Sodbury lie part in the wolds and part on the scarp edge. Chipping Sodbury, in the vale to the west, is the largest and the most recent of the three villages. Originally, Old Sodbury had been the principal market here, but its site on the hill restricted further expansion. The solution was to establish a new town and market at what is now Chipping Sodbury in 1277. Old Sodbury (755815) is perhaps a little spoiled by having the main A432 sweep through it, but there are a few good buildings tucked up the side lanes. Little Sodbury (758832) is little more than a few houses and farm buildings with the exception of the rather stark and restored manor house. On the hill behind the village and visible from the A46(T) to the east as serrated ramparts on the edge of the hill are the well-preserved remains of an Iron-Age hillfort: in its way Little Sodbury combines in a small way those features of archaeology, architecture and landscape characteristic of the south Cotswolds more generally.

CHAPTER 21

Bath, Bradford-on-Avon, and the Avon Valley

The natural landscape of the southern Cotswolds is dramatic enough, especially the western fringes of the wolds. But in Bath, the landscape, equally dramatic, is man-made. One historian has considered the town 'the greatest public work of art in eighteenth-century England'. The principal medium of Bath as a work of art is Cotswolds stone, taken from quarries at Box and Corsham. There is, of course, more to Bath than its surviving eighteenth-century buildings, but in discovering the town the visitor is almost everywhere confronted with evidence of the town's 'Golden Age', and the town trail that follows pays particular attention to this Georgian 'New' town.

Early settlement in the Bath area was centred on the hillfort of Little Solsbury (768679), situated on a spur of the wolds overlooking the modern town. The first recorded name for the town is 'Aquae Sulis', given by the Romans in about AD 65 to an already-existing shrine and spring in honour of the Celtic deity Sulis. Roman Bath was dominated by the Sanctuary of Sulis Minerva with the hot springs and baths attracting people from the European mainland as well as throughout Roman Britain. For all its importance as a Roman tourist resort, Roman Bath was relatively small in comparison with the much more important civic capital of Corinium. Given this importance and the later development of Bath as a spa in the eighteenth century, it is surprising that, apart from a few minor finds in intervening centuries and more notable discoveries of Roman architecture during rebuilding in the 1790s, Roman Bath remained almost entirely forgotten until the later nineteenth century. Excavations in 1867 and 1889 for new spa buildings revealed the extent of the Roman town, although much remains to be known of Bath at that period. It is something of a paradox, too, that efforts to revive a facility by then in serious decline should for the first time reveal the evidence for a spa that had made Bath famous about two thousand years before.

The Roman Baths and Pump Room Museum a little west of

The Abbey Church and precinct in Bath, from an early nineteenth-century engraving by an unknown artist.

the Abbey Church offer among the best evidence of Bath's use of the local hot springs in both Roman and Georgian times. The West Baths here are amongst the best-preserved Roman remains in Europe and the Museum takes the visitor on a well-thought-out route from evidence for early settlement in the area through to the extensive Roman remains. The Pump Room, at which the waters may be tasted, was built in 1796, one of the very last buildings to be erected under Bath's Improvement Act of 1789. The connection between Roman Bath and the town in its heyday as a spa resort in the eighteenth century extends to more than this shared devotion to the waters. And to understand the connection properly, one must turn to the intervening centuries, if only briefly.

Though not unimportant as a town in the Saxon period – indeed, the town held the then equivalent of Parliament, the 'Witan', in 901 – Bath lay for a long time within the bounds of the older Roman town. The town was sacked by Normans in 1088. As so often, destruction then was a later boon. A massive cathedral church was begun in 1091 roughly situated where the Abbey Church is now. The town expanded during the medieval period as a market and ecclesiastical centre to fill the area roughly bounded today by the west end of Westgate Street (the site of the western entrance to Bath), and the Lower and Upper Borough Walls to the south and north respectively. Therein lay a problem. By about 1700 (and despite some extramural building beyond the town's Northgate), Bath was effectively full up. Building had to take place beyond the confines of the old town. And it is this new Bath of the eighteenth century that provides the link with the town in the Roman period: the new town was intended to be a new Rome.

Bath's expansion and self-creation as an eighteenth-century work of art has three main phases. The first dates from 1725 to about 1758 and includes, most notably, the work of John Wood. The second, from about 1762 to 1774, also saw development at the hands of a John Wood, this time the son, the elder Wood having died in 1754. The third phase dates from 1775 to 1796, especially from 1789. The results of each and the combined effect can be followed in the trail below. From the Abbey Church or the Roman Baths, go a little way up Milsom Street before turning first left along Quiet Street and, from there, into Wood Street. Continuing along Wood Street will bring you into Queen's Square at its south-east corner.

Queen's Square, designed by Wood Senior and begun late in 1728, is magnificent. It is, simultaneously, one of the finest examples of the Palladian style in Britain with all the balance, harmony and proportion that this implies, and part of the new Rome that, then, was Bath. In his plans for the town, Wood spoke of how he '... proposed to make a grand Place of Assembly, to be called the Royal Forum of Bath ... another Place ... to be called the Grand Circus ... and a third Place ... to be called the Imperial Gymnasium of the City, from a Work of that Kind, taking its Rise at first in Bath, during the Time of the Roman Emperors'. From the uniform splendour of Queen's Square (where lived Dr William Oliver, inventor of the biscuit that bears both his name and that of his town), go uphill and along Gay Street. At the top, you enter The Circus.

The Circus was the third of Wood Senior's great designs for Bath (the second being the now much-spoilt Abbey Orchard, the intended site of the never-built Great Forum), but he never lived to see it finished. The Circus was completed by his son in 1758. It is easy to see, even now, how this essay in form and order would have been seen then as part of a new empire: look above the front doors – the finely-styled sheaves of wheat and other agricultural produce symbolise the agrarian wealth that underwrote this new urbanism. From The Circus, the street on the left is Brock Street. Go along it to arrive at Royal Crescent.

More than one scholar has considered Royal Crescent to be 'the most perfect essay in urban architecture in the western world'. Lovers of Georgian Edinburgh might quibble, but Royal Crescent, designed by Wood the Younger and built between 1767 and 1774, is incomparable not only for its sense of balance and symmetry but for its outstanding position. Number 1 Royal Crescent is open to the public and shows, in decor and furnishings, what one of these houses would have looked like in the late eighteenth century. From Royal Crescent, go back down Brock Street and round The Circus into Bennett Street. The Assembly Rooms here, built between 1768 and 1771, house a Museum of Costume. From here, go downhill along Bartlett Street and take a right turn into the top end of Milsom Street.

One commentator on Bath in the late 1830s wrote that 'Trade in Bath consists principally in the sale of articles connected with the refinements, rather than the necessities of life'. Looking at the shops in Milsom Street and elsewhere 150 years later, it is hard to disagree. Milsom Street and Union Street to its south effectively connect the last phase of the development of Georgian Bath with the earlier ones. By the end of the eighteenth century (and symbolised in the Pump Room), Bath had superb buildings for functions no longer fashionable there.

From Abbey Orchard, the graceful lines of the Pulteney Bridge, built between 1769 and 1774, can be seen to good advantage. Cross over the Avon into Argyle Street and from Laura Place into Great Pulteney Street. These streets are the work of Thomas Baldwin between 1788 and 1790. The intention was to make the east side of the river as grand as Wood's Upper Town but bankruptcy halted the plans before completion. At the east end of Great Pulteney Street in Sydney Gardens, the Holbourne Museum and Crafts Centre has collections of eighteenth-century porcelain and silver and work by contemporary artists. Further to the east (take the car and

follow the A36(T) signposted Warminster or go over
Bathampton Down past Bath University), is the American
Museum at Claverton Manor (789641). The Museum was
begun in 1961, and since that time has built up extensive
displays of American life and material culture presented in
rooms that take the visitor from the seventeenth to the
nineteenth centuries.

Bath is a contradiction. It is a vibrant and well-to-do modern
town and a museum of the eighteenth century like no other. At
the same time as the Woods and Baldwin and others were
constructing their Palladian terraces and squares for the better-
off, streets like Avon Street housed an impoverished under-
class riddled with disease. Genteel, almost courtly leisure,
centred around spa, theatre, and coffee rooms was paralleled
by a lively trade in pornographic publishing. Spas went out of
fashion just as buildings provided for them were finished. And
parts of medieval Bath survived Georgian expansion only to be
knocked down in the 1950s by people who call themselves
professional planners. Yet, contradiction or not, Bath remains
a delight. Apart from those features mentioned already, there
is an Industrial Centre, a Postal Museum, a Geology Museum, a
wonderful theatre in the Theatre Royal, a good Art Gallery in
Bridge Street (the topographical views of Thomas Malton are
particularly fine), and at The Boathouse (north off the A36(T)
from Sydney Gardens) and at Monkton Combe on the Midford
Brook (773618), boats may be hired.

North and east of Bath, the A4(T) leads towards Box and
Corsham, the former itself a spa of sorts before competition
from Bath ended the town's hopes in the early nineteenth
century. Both are better known for their quarries, Box stone
being particularly widely-used in the south Cotswolds. Between
the two towns, HMS Royal Arthur, south of Moor Green
(852682), is a naval store occupying the site of the former
Corsham Down quarries. Corsham Court (874705) is, in
original plan, a late sixteenth-century manor house extended in
the nineteenth century. The Court houses a superb collection
of paintings and furniture. The gardens, which sweep down to
an extensive lake at the east, are the work of Capability Brown
and have lovely trees. At Monkton Farleigh (805652), former
quarries used as wartime ammunition dumps are open to the

Bradford-on-Avon with the modern bridge near Westbury House spanning the river to lead to the Saxon chapel of St. Lawrence and The Tory beyond.

public. East of here, the manor house at South Wraxall (833653) is perhaps less grand than Corsham Court, but it is a splendid example of a clothier's mansion from the later sixteenth century.

East of Bath along the Avon Valley, the river is followed for much of the way by the Kennet and Avon Canal. This was begun in 1794 and completed in 1810. Before being bought up by the Great Western Railway in the 1850s, from which time the carriage of goods declined greatly, the canal was a principal means of transporting quarry stone. Former canal wharves can still be seen south of Turleigh (806604).

In its way, Bradford-on-Avon (825614) outshines Bath. Both reveal themselves in their buildings: Bath's terraces and ornamented grace testify to a leisured past and a present wealth: Bradford-on-Avon's buildings, smaller, less ornate and with a very different purpose, reflect the town's past rôle as the centre of the south Cotswolds woollen industry. The town is still an industrial centre today as the Avon Rubber Company has its headquarters here, but neither this modern use nor the buildings that house it detract from the charm of this little town.

The old core of Bradford centres around narrow lanes and streets north of the Town Bridge, the site of that earlier 'broad ford' which gives the town its name, and the buildings immediately south of the river. The Town Bridge is a good place from which to view the rows of weavers' cottages and other buildings to the north that give the town its particular character, and is a central point, too, from which to explore Bradford. The present bridge is, in part, medieval – two arches on the eastern side date from the thirteenth century – but it mostly dates from the seventeenth century. The small building on the eastern side was originally a chapel belonging to the former St Margaret's Hospital, a leper hospice run by Shaftesbury Abbey in Dorset, but it was used from the seventeenth century as the town prison.

Cross the Town Bridge to the south. The buildings on the corner of St Margaret's Street (the site of the early medieval hospital) and Bridge Street are clothiers' houses of the seventeenth century; some still have the remains of workshops in their backyards. Continuing down Bridge Street will bring you to a number of later cloth mills, in origin mid-eighteenth century, but later altered on several occasions to incorporate new machinery. From here, the present factories of the Avon Rubber Company can be seen on the other bank. Rubber manufacture has been an industry in Bradford since 1848. Retrace your steps and turn left along St Margaret's Street. At this point, the visitor can decide on a choice of routes and things to see in Bradford. All can easily be walked: the path across the river to the Saxon chapel and up the hill to St Mary Tory and the cottages and views here can only be walked from this point. The other options are either to go along St Margaret's Street and then into Frome Street towards the locks and wharves on the Kennet and Avon Canal or follow the path along the south bank of the Avon towards Barton Farm. In fact, it is easy enough to do all of these things, and those with a mind to can continue the walk along the Avon as far as Avoncliff and come into Bradford on the north bank along the minor road south of Turleigh. Belcombe Court on the western fringes of Bradford here was extensively remodelled by Wood the Elder; the result is said to have pleased him as much as anything he designed in Bath.

The building on the corner of St Margaret's Street is Westbury House, a clothier's house but on a grander scale altogether than many in the town. In 1791, the area in front of this house was the scene of a riot by labourers in Bradford's cloth industries. The owner of Westbury House, the mill-owner Joseph Phelps, had introduced a scribbling machine into his mills in an effort to improve production and quality. Fearful of the loss of their jobs (rightly so as it later turned out), workers rioted, dragged the new machinery to the Town Bridge, and, despite being shot at by Phelps and others (with the loss of three lives), burnt the machine there. Scribbling by machinery went ahead anyway: the charge against Phelps was 'justifiable homicide'.

From Westbury House, continue along the riverside walk towards Barton Farm. (If going via Frome Street and the canal, follow the signs to the farm down Pound Lane.) The buildings at Barton Farm today date from the early fourteenth century, but there has been a manor farm here on land owned by Shaftesbury Abbey since 1001 until the dissolution of their holdings in 1539. The Farm now has a farmhouse, a granary, and a superb tithe barn, one of the largest in the country, with very well-preserved roof timbers and two massive entrances. The solid and wide Packbridge or Barton Bridge here crosses the river where old trade routes brought tithe goods to be stored in the barn. Go over the bridge, and, taking care because the footpath crosses the railway, continue up the path as it runs between high walls to lead into Barton Orchard.

The houses in this part of Bradford date from the mid-seventeenth century and later. The streets of Barton Orchard, Middle Rank, Newtown and Tory were all built to house cloth workers and their families as Bradford's textile industries expanded during this period. Paul Methuen, a Bradford clothier with trade connections with the Low Countries and Spain (his descendants later bought and still own Corsham Court), introduced skilled workers from Amsterdam to Bradford in 1659. The area around the parish church is still known locally as Dutch Barton. Go along Barton Orchard and, at the end, either turn down Church Street towards the parish church, the Saxon chapel and the river, or, leaving those until later, go up Barton Steps and Well Path towards the streets of Middle Rank, Tory, and the chapel of St Mary Tory.

Both Middle Rank Tory and Top Rank Tory have weavers' cottages and more substantial eighteenth-century townhouses in splendid states of repair. The chapel of St Mary Tory was built about 1480 as a pilgrims' resthouse, but, like the chapel on the Townbridge, has been put to alternative use in the past, in this case as a textile workshop. The view from the chapel out over the town and, on good days, to the Mendips and the Wiltshire Downs, is well worth the effort of getting to the top. As with other sites along the Cotswolds' edge, it was this position that attracted Iron-Age settlers to build a hillfort here. Nothing remains today of this very first Bradford.

From the chapel, make your way downhill and along Newtown to turn right down Market Street. The Priory Barn at the end of Newtown is a restored fifteenth-century building now used as a hall. As you turn down Market Street, look across to your left at the cottage on the bend in the road. Attractively situated, this thatched Victorian cottage loses something of its picturesque charm in having modern stonework for the window surrounds. The bottom end of Market Street is set round with a number of seventeenth- and eighteenth-century buildings, some spoilt by later frontages. From here, go along Church Street, keeping an eye out for Old Church House and Druce's Hill House, both good examples of clothiers' houses, from the early sixteenth and early eighteenth centuries respectively.

The Church of Holy Trinity owes its size and style to wealth generated by townsfolk in the wool trade and cloth industries. The chantry in the east end, for example, was founded by Thomas Horton whose house, Old Church House, can be seen in Church Street. A memorial brass to the man himself is situated in the north aisle. Fine as Holy Trinity is, it perhaps pales in comparison (and certainly does in terms of historical significance) with the Saxon chapel of St Lawrence opposite. This dates to the time of Aldhelm the first Abbot of Malmesbury between about AD 675 and 705 and is an extraordinary, and fortunate, survival. Until about 1856, no one even knew it was there. It was surrounded by houses, had been altered by the insertion of a chimney (where the chancel arch is now), had windows, and, as though that were not enough, had been divided into two separate dwellings: the nave, itself separated into upper and lower storeys, had a school in the upper room; the chancel was a cottage. The discovery of the carved angels now high on the wall above the chancel arch led to the eventual discovery of the chapel as a whole. The fact that the chimney had used the original masonry meant that the chapel could be, in part, re-assembled as well as restored. It is a lovely, plain and quiet place and an extremely important Saxon survival. From here, the path leads downhill to a footbridge over the river. (Those who have come to the chapel first can follow the above route in reverse.) As you pass over the bridge, look across at the two mills, Abbey Mill and Church Street Mill, on the north bank of the Avon. Abbey Mill, which dates from 1874 and has been restored by the Avon Rubber Company, was the last mill to be built in Bradford. Its Gothick style, interesting in itself, does not fit very well with the other buildings in the town but it is good that it has survived. The path leads back to Westbury House.

Within easy reach of Bradford are two very fine manor houses. Great Chalfield Manor (860632), which can be reached on minor roads north of the B3107 Melksham Road, is a splendid example of a moated manor house. Westwood Manor, in Westwood village (812592) a little to the south-west of Bradford, is largely the work of Thomas Horton, the Bradford clothier whose house and brass we have already noted. Both the manor houses and Bradford-on-Avon itself look south towards the hills and vales of Somerset and Wiltshire, although they stand on the very fringes of the Cotswolds.

CHAPTER 22

Beyond the Cotswolds' Edge

Concluding a book on discovering the Cotswolds with a chapter on places of interest to visit beyond the area may seem strange. And so it is, in that there is so much to see and do in the Cotswolds themselves. That's the trouble with regions: they have boundaries and there is always something of interest just that little bit further on. The majority of the places mentioned in what follows lie within one hour's drive of the Cotswolds' edge (depending on quite where you start from, of course). Gloucester, the Forest of Dean, the water garden at Westbury-on-Severn, Tewkesbury, Great Malvern and the Malvern Hills, Stratford-upon-Avon are all easily reached from the north Cotswolds. Salisbury and Winchester, Glastonbury, the Somerset Levels and other places to see in the vales and on the plains south of Marlborough are quite easy to get to from the south Cotswolds. But neither these and other places nor some of the larger towns – Oxford, Bristol, Cheddar Gorge, Warwick Castle, Hereford and the Black Mountains of the Welsh Borders beyond Ross-on-Wye and Monmouth, for example – can receive more than passing mention here.

Gloucester has much to offer visitors, but nothing the equal of its cathedral whose 225-foot-high tower is visible from many points along the north-west scarp edge. A church has stood on this site since 681, but the present building in most part dates from 1089 and was planned by Serlo, the first Norman abbot. The church was formally consecrated in 1121 but construction and reconstruction, of associated monastic buildings as well as the Abbey Church (which properly became a Cathedral only in 1541), continued throughout the twelfth and thirteenth centuries. The result of this and later work – the present tower dates from 1450, for example, and there was extensive restoration in 1616, 1847 and 1953 – is a magnificent monument to the glory of God. The Cathedral can claim to be the birthplace of Perpendicular architecture: the south window is the first surviving window to have been built in the style (c.1335). The glorious east window, with its commemoration of knights who fought at Crécy and Calais, was probably finished by 1350 – no mean achievement given the then widespread effect of the plague. The colours and detail of form are lovely, the breadth of vision in the undertaking awe-inspiring. Everywhere the skills of medieval craftsmen endure: in the fan-vaulting, in the alabaster and marble tomb of Edward II, in the massive Norman columns in the nave.

In the Cathedral precinct there are monastic and other buildings of interest, notably the Great Cloister. In an earlier Chapter House here, William the Conqueror gave orders in 1086 to begin the survey known to us now as the Domesday Book. Other medieval sites of interest in Gloucester include the remains of the Dominican friary – Black Friars – on Southgate Street, and, less extensively, of Llanthony Priory, built in 1136 as a daughter house to Llanthony St John in Wales. Llanthony Priory may be reached via Hempstead Lane/Severn Road south-west from Gloucester Docks.

The National Waterways Museum in the converted Llanthony warehouse at Gloucester Docks has excellent displays about the Canal Age and trade along the Gloucester-Berkeley Canal as well as working machinery and boats. Less exciting for children perhaps, but well worth a visit, is the Museum of Advertising and Packaging in the Albert Warehouse. Boat trips and dock tours are also available. Other museums worth a visit are the Folk Museum in Westgate Street (the building is a fine example of Tudor domestic architecture), the City Museum and Art Gallery, and the City East Gate Museum with its displays from Gloucester's Roman past. Both these museums are within easy walking distance down Westgate and Eastgate Streets from the Cathedral.

One of the more spectacular sites in the local area is the Severn Bore, that 'moving wall' of water evident at various times of the year. A bore is a surging wave formed at the foremost part of tides that run into river channels of roughly funnel shape. The local press should give the best days and times to see the Severn Bore, which is easily the largest on several British rivers. The Bore begins to form near Sharpness: there are good viewing points at Stonebench on the eastern bank, Minsterworth and several places on the west bank or on

Telford's bridge at Over, just west of Gloucester on the A40.

Westbury Court Garden in Westbury-on-Severn, on the A48(T) Gloucester to Chepstow road, is a small but extremely attractive water garden laid out in the Dutch manner in 1696. Now managed by the National Trust, the garden has ornate topiary and a geometric parterre characteristic of garden planning before the informal layouts of landscape gardeners like Launcelot 'Capability' Brown and Humphrey Repton became accepted fashion. It is a rare and lovely survival. Those interested in gardens may like to compare the formality of design at Westbury Court with either the open scene of Repton's garden at Blaise Castle near Henbury on the north-west fringes of Bristol (take junction 17 of the M5), or the informality of nearby Blaise Hamlets village. The remarkable cottages here, each different from the other, were built in 1810 to house elderly estate labourers. Blaise Hamlets is the finest example in buildings of the Picturesque movement in the country. Other lovely gardens within easy reach of the Cotswolds are Rousham, just east of the A423(T) Oxford-Banbury road at its junction with the B4030 south of Steeple Aston, and the gardens at Blenheim Palace, a little further south near Woodstock. Rousham is the work of William Kent (1685-1748) and is one of the very few gardens of the period to escape alteration. The gardens at Blenheim, seat of the Dukes of Marlborough and birthplace of Sir Winston Churchill, are the combined result of successive work by Wise, Vanbrugh, and most especially, Capability Brown.

On the west bank of the Severn estuary between Gloucester and Chepstow lies that 'little country on its own', the Forest of Dean. The Forest was a major industrial region in the past: iron ore and coal were worked in the bloomeries, timber was used for charcoal, 'steweries' produced wood-based chemicals, and Lydney was once a major port and shipbuilding town. Relics of this industrial past are everywhere. The Dean Heritage Centre at Soudley near Cinderford (signposted on the B4227 from Blakeney) has exhibitions and a reconstructed mine and working smallholding. At the Clearwell caves (off the B4231 from Lydney) there are caverns left by centuries of mining with displays illustrating how ore has been mined. The Forest has waymarked trails for walkers, and the longer-distance footpaths of the Wye Valley walk and Offa's Dyke Footpath run along the west and east banks of the River Wye north of Chepstow. At Newent in the north-east of the Forest, there is a Butterfly Centre, a museum of Victorian life in 'The Shambles', and a Falconry Centre where magnificent and rare birds of prey are trained and studied as part of important conservation programmes. Together with the Wye Valley (although Tintern Abbey is now much spoiled by the pressures of mass tourism and no longer the scene of what William Wordsworth in 1798 considered 'tranquil restoration'), the Forest of Dean is a fascinating area well worth a prolonged visit.

In Tewkesbury, site of the battle in 1471 which effectively ended the Lancastrian cause in the Wars of the Roses, the Abbey Church of St Mary should command the greatest attention from the visitor. The nave of the present building is contemporary with that at Gloucester Cathedral. The glass here is earlier, though not by much, than that in Gloucester. Amongst St Mary's many delights, the vermin shown gnawing the corpse on the Wakeman Cenotaph are a wonderful representation of the medieval preoccupation with death. Hemmed in as it is by the Swilgate River on the south and the Avon and Severn to the west, Tewkesbury has retained a number of half-timbered medieval buildings within its constricted site as well as many dwellings of later age in its winding alleys, themselves the result of the lack of room for development.

South of Tewkesbury and off a minor road from the B4213 is the village of Deerhurst. St Mary's here, parts of which date from 804, is one of the finest Anglo-Saxon churches in Britain. Its detailed building history is complex and has been the focus of several recent excavations and surveys, but the surviving evidence is no less remarkable for its complexity. The font is considered by some to be the finest Saxon font in existence and has Celtic motifs in addition. Other delights are the carved heads in the entrance door and the Deerhurst Angel carved in the arch of the apse. Down the lane toward the river is Odda's Chapel, the remains of another Anglo-Saxon church (dedicated by Ealdred in 1056), not 'discovered' until 1885 and not restored until 1965.

North-west of the Cotswolds and across the vale in which
Tewkesbury stands are the Malvern Hills, which separate the
counties of Hereford and Worcester. The highest point,
Worcestershire Beacon, to the north end of the eight-mile
ridge, affords wonderful views, and there are many paths,
some steep, as well as the main footpath which runs the length
of the hills. In the past, visiting dignitaries, including royalty,
made the ascent on donkeys, kept in large number by
Malvern's 'donkey women'. The line of what Celia Fiennes in
1696 called hills 'in Pirramidy fashion' is broken in two places
by the flatter summits of Iron-Age hillforts at Midsummer Hill
and Herefordshire Beacon, the latter also known as British
Camp.

Great Malvern was centred around a Benedictine Priory,
founded in 1085. Little remains of it now. Modern Malvern,
like Cheltenham, Bath, and Royal Leamington Spa to the
north-east, owes its growth to the exploitation of its waters. Like
Cheltenham, where Dr Short's treatise on the waters helped
establish the town's popularity, Malvern owes much to a Dr
John Wall whose 1757 work on Malvern's waters claimed that
people would benefit from its purity: 'The Malvern Water, says
Dr John Wall, is famed for containing just nothing at all'. And
as Cheltenham has Gustav Holst, so Malvern has its composer
in Edward Elgar who moved there in 1889 and who wrote both
the *Dream of Gerontius* and the *Enigma Variations* here.

Worcester, only a few miles from Malvern, has a lovely
Cathedral (perhaps best seen from the cricket ground across
the Severn), and other interesting historic buildings including
the Commandery, which was the Royalist headquarters towards
the end of the Civil War. From Worcester, the A422 runs
eastwards towards Stratford-upon-Avon which may also be
reached from Cheltenham and the Cotswolds via Evesham and
the A46. The flat landscape of the Vale of Evesham with its
productive fruit growing is broken by the isolated rise of
Bredon Hill. From the top on a summer's day, it is indeed
possible, as A. E. Housman wrote, to 'see the coloured
counties, And hear the larks so high'.

Stratford-upon-Avon is the birthplace of William
Shakespeare. With its theatres for the Royal Shakespeare
Company, Shakespeare's birthplace in Henley Street (now a

museum), and the Shakespeare Centre, the town owes a lot to a man who spent much of his working life in London. Stratford is one of the most visited places in Britain; but there is as much to enjoy (and certainly more quietly) in the surrounding countryside. Compton Wynyates, built about 1520 and, for many, the 'jewel in the crown' of sixteenth-century mansions, lies south-east of Stratford (take the A34(T) to Shipston-on-Stour when coming from the Cotswolds). Charlcote, east of Stratford on the B4056, was built in 1558 and has a fine gatehouse.

Henry James wrote that 'Oxford lends sweetness to labour and dignity to leisure'. Oxford is best known for its university, many of whose colleges are built of Cotswold stone, but while labour within these buildings may be sweet, it is not always easy to take one's leisure with dignity in the summer months. Most of the colleges have guided tours and the university Botanic Garden (east end of the High Street) offers some relief from crowds.

Beyond the south-east edge of the Cotswolds, the landscape opens and flattens towards the Vale of the White Horse and the Vale of Pewsey before rising again as the downlands of Salisbury Plain. Silbury Hill and the stone circle at Avebury (both west of Marlborough on the A4 and A361) are within quite easy reach of the southern Cotswolds. Stonehenge, Woodhenge, Old Sarum, and the Cathedral and other attractions in and near Salisbury take longer to get to. The countryside and buildings here have a character very different from that of the Cotswolds – in the use of thatch for roofing material, for example – and towards the wetlands of the Somerset Levels south of the Mendips, the landscape changes again.

Guide to Further Reading

Among a number of general guides to the Cotswolds are:
J. Finberg, *The Cotswolds* (London, 1976).
C. & A. M. Hadfield (eds.), *The Cotswolds: a new study* (Newton Abbot, 1973).
B. Smith *The Cotswolds* (London, 1976).

The definitive guide to the buildings of the Cotswolds is:
D. Verey, *Gloucestershire: The Cotswolds* (in the *Buildings of England* series, ed. by N. Pevsner) (First edition 1970; reprinted with corrections 1989).

For places in the vale and the Oxfordshire wolds mentioned here, see:
D. Verey, *Gloucestershire: The Vale and the Forest of Dean* (in the *Buildings of England* series) (First edition 1970; reprinted with corrections 1980).
J. Sherwood & N. Pevsner, *Oxfordshire* (the *Buildings of England* series) (London, 1974).

Also interesting on buildings, though for a prescribed area within the Cotswolds as a whole, is:
N. H. Cooper (ed.), *The Cirencester Area* (London, 1988).

On archaeology and history, a comprehensive guide with a good bibliography is:
A. Saville (ed.), *Archaeology in Gloucestershire* (Gloucester, 1984).

Two good guides to archaeological sites include:
RCHM (Royal Commission on Historical Monuments), *Iron Age and Romano-British Monuments in the Gloucestershire Cotswolds* (London, 1976).
A. Saville, *Archaeological sites in the Avon and Gloucestershire Cotswolds: an extensive survey of a rural archaeological resource with special reference to plough damage* (Bristol, 1980).

On the Roman Cotswolds, see:
K. Branigan & P. Fowler (eds.), *The Roman West Country: classical culture and Celtic society* (Newton Abbot, 1976).
A. McWhirr, *Roman Gloucestershire* (Gloucester, 1981).

Two general historical accounts with good attention to the making of the Cotswold landscape are:
H. P. R. Finberg (ed.), *Gloucestershire Studies* (Leicester, 1957).
H. P. R. Finberg, *The Gloucestershire Landscape* (London, 1975).

On place names, the best reference for the Cotswolds is vol. 2. of A. H. Smith, *The Place Names of Gloucestershire* (4 volumes, Cambridge, 1964-65).

On tradition and folklore, see:
K. Briggs, *The Folklore of the Cotswolds* (London, 1975).
E. Brill, *Life and Tradition on the Cotswolds* (London, 1974).

On industrial archaeology, see:
W. Awdry (ed.), *Industrial Archaeology in Gloucestershire* (Third edition, Dursley, 1983).

Some of the above books devote space to the Cotswolds woollen industry as part of their general accounts of the area; more specific attention is given in:
J. de L. Mann, *The Cloth Industry in the West of England from 1640 to 1880* (First edition Oxford, 1971: reprinted Gloucester, 1987).
K. Ponting, *The Woollen Industry of South West England* (Bath, 1971)
J. Tann, *Gloucestershire Woollen Mills* (Newton Abbot, 1967).

On transport in the Cotswolds, see:
D. J. Viner, *Transport in the Cotswolds from old photographs* (Nelson, 1981).

And as guides to the walks by which to discover the Cotswolds, see:
M. Handford & D. J. Viner, *Stroudwater and Thames and Severn Canals Towpath Guide* (Gloucester, 1984).

P. A. Price, *Walks for Motorists: Cotswolds – Northern Area* (London, 1979).

P. A. Price, *Walks for Motorists: Cotswolds – Southern Area* (London, 1979).

M. Richards, *The Cotswold Way* (London, 1984).

Index